The

Commander William Don
in Keswick in 1910 a
saw service on the China sta
Second World War, relayed h
who saw incessant action th
hostilities. He was invalided out of the Royal Navy in 1948
and returned to live in Cumberland. He died in 2002.

STAND BY FOR ACTION

COMMANDER WILLIAM DONALD
DSC AND BAR

Seaforth
PUBLISHING

Copyright © William Donald 1956
Introduction Copyright © Richard Woodman 2009

First published in Great Britain in 2009 by
Seaforth Publishing,
Pen & Sword Books Ltd,
47 Church Street,
Barnsley S70 2AS

www.seaforthpublishing.com

British Library Cataloguing in Publication Data
A catalogue record for this book is available from the British Library

ISBN 978 1 84832 016 1

First published by William Kimber & Co Ltd in 1956

Printed and bound in Great Britain by CPI Bookmarque, Croydon, Surrey

CONTENTS

Part One
NORWAY

CONTENTS

PART FIVE

OPERATION 'OVERLORD'

EPILOGUE

WAR TO PEACE

To
all those shipmates with whom,
through many an adventure, it
was my good fortune and
privilege to serve.

INTRODUCTION

A	S A NAVAL memoir of the Second World War, this is a remarkably self-effacing account from which the author emerges as a brave, decent and frank individual; and the lack of postwar glorification makes it a fascinating and very honest account of one naval officer's war experiences. What adds particular value is that Donald spent much of his war in what, at least in the perception of mainstream naval history, is something of a backwater.

Donald makes little mention of his life in the service prior to the outbreak of hostilities. He was, in fact, born at Keswick, Cumberland, on 1 July 1910. His father had served as mayor of Carlisle and, after Dartmouth, Midshipman William Spooner Donald was sent to serve the empire in small men-of-war, mainly on the China station. At the beginning of 1939 he was back in Britain and, with the shadow of conflict looming in the months after Munich, he and nine other lieutenants were sent to Whale Island prior to taking up appointments as first lieutenants in newly commissioning destroyers and sloops. Donald passed out tenth, but was satisfied that he had "jumped the first hurdle" to command. He joined HM sloop *Black Swan* and, under Captain A L Poland DSC, was part of the Rosyth Escort Force whose main task was the protection of convoys up and down the coast from Methil to the Thames. This was in due course to be the theatre in which Donald spent the greater part of the War, but for the *Black Swan*'s involvement in the Norwegian campaign. What became a costly débâcle was no fault of the forces engaged, and the *Black Swan* was under intermittent air attack as she provided anti-aircraft defence to troops ashore, actually sustaining a bomb-hit in her stern which fortunately failed to detonate, though it drove several holes right through three decks and a bulkhead on its passage through the lucky ship. For his services in Norway, Donald was awarded the DSC.

The *Black Swan* resumed the task of escorting east coast convoys which, in addition to consisting of coasters carrying general cargoes and colliers with much needed coal for power-stations, industry and domestic consumption in the south of England, also included the deep-water merchantmen dispersed from trans-atlantic convoys with cargoes consigned to those few east coast ports—including London—that were still able to handle the discharge of their lading in defiance of the German blitz. These convoys, which proceeded through swept channels marked by dimly lit buoys at intervals of five miles, commonly consisted of fifty ships in close order. In shallow water off the East Anglian coast, obstructed by numerous shoals and subject to fierce tides, the task would have been difficult enough in those pre-radar days, but to the further natural complications of foul weather with gales at one end of the spectrum and oily, foggy calms at the other, there were the added risks of enemy action.

Spotting aircraft could call up Luftwaffe units, usually Junkers Ju88s, which attacked by day, while at night the convoys, trundling along their predictable routes at seven knots could easily be interdicted by fast, heavily armed German E-boats. Frequent sallies were made by the enemy in order to outwit the efforts of the tireless minesweepers, and mines accounted for many vessels, further complicating the convoys' navigation by littering the fair-way with wrecks.

In due course—and after *Black Swan* had herself encountered a mine—Donald was promoted to lieutenant commander and appointed as captain to HMS *Guillemot*, a small, elegant Bird-class corvette which was also part of the Rosyth Escort Force. In *Guillemot* he continued the dull but dangerous task of working up and down the east coast. Although enemy attack was not inevitable, the risk of interception was constant, hence the title of his memoir, *Stand by for Action*, and Donald's text is eloquent of the fatigue induced by constant vigilance, fatigue which easily turned into exhaustion. He is candid enough to admit his own funda-mental errors when things went wrong, and his book is a text for any would-be ship's captain, shorn of the glories and dwelling upon the realities of life in a small warship with its sparse pleasures and grindingly monotonous routines. There is no word of complaint and he devotes a section to the essential development of Coastal Forces and the gallantry of men like

Lieutenant Commander R P Hichens who took the battle to the enemy.

Notwithstanding his modesty, Donald was clearly a dedicated and thoroughly professional sea-officer, a fact recognised by Their Lordships, who next appointed him to the old V-Class destroyer *Verdun*, also part of the Rosyth Escort Force. Towards the end of the War Donald was transferred to command the new destroyer HMS *Ulster* in which, leading his squadron, he was engaged in a fierce engagement in the Western Channel with three German destroyers, an action which earned him a bar to his DSC. Later service in the Mediterranean confirmed his skill as a destroyer commander and he was present at the Anzio landings before being withdrawn prior to the assault on Normandy on D-Day in June 1944. His description of Operation Neptune is particularly vivid but he was now under great strain, suffering from battle-fatigue and requested to be relieved of his command.

In due course, however, he was appointed second-in-command of HMS *Glengyle*, a fine, fast cargo-liner which had been converted to an infantry assault vessel. Fortunately, rather than landing troops on the Japanese coast, the dropping of the atomic bomb found *Glengyle* repatriating internees from Hong Kong. Donald's end-of-war foray into the eastern seas on such a mission was clearly an emotional experience for him and brings out the humanity for which he was admired by his young ship's companies. He possessed an uncanny sense of premonition which saved lives on several occasions and which he was unable to account for.

After the War and promoted to commander, Donald commanded HM destroyer *Concord* before being invalided out of the Royal Navy in 1948 on account of debilitating deafness, probably brought on by exposure to frequent gunfire. He returned to his wife and daughter in his beloved Cumberland to run a business, where he died in 2002.

This book was a bestselling autobiography on its appearance in 1956 and retains a freshness and humanity which is a lasting testimony to its author.

Captain Richard Woodman FRHistS FNI
Author of the three convoy histories,
Arctic Convoys, *Malta Convoys* and the *Real Cruel Sea*

PART ONE

NORWAY

CHAPTER I

INTO ACTION

THE FIRST few months of 1939 I spent at Portsmouth Barracks as a member of the Training staff for New Entry Seamen. Life was peaceful and pleasant, and I played hockey twice a week for Portsmouth Services and the Navy hockey teams. My wife and I had just settled into a little house in Alverstoke, and the outlook in every way was quite promising.

But as the first rumbles of the approaching war gradually made themselves heard, retired officers were called up for the shore jobs, and all available active service officers like myself were appointed to ships.

"Nice job for you anyway, Donald," said the Training Commander one April morning, "Number One of a new sloop building."

"Where, sir?"

"*Black Swan*—up at Yarrow's in Bonnie Scotland."

Before going up to Clydeside, I had to do a three-weeks' gunnery course at Whale Island. Ten of us took the course—all First Lieutenants of new destroyers and sloops then being built. I passed out tenth: but I had the satisfaction of knowing that I had jumped the first hurdle towards a destroyer command.

When I arrived at Yarrow's, the *Black Swan* had not even been launched, and the Engineer Officer was the only other officer as yet appointed. "Chiefee" Germain was a Lieutenant (E) ex-Lower Deck, and a good deal older than myself. He was very efficient at his job, and we got on very well together. We shared an office with our opposite numbers of the *Flamingo*, sister ship of the *Black Swan*, but in a more advanced state of completion. Two other ships were also being built there, the destroyers *Jupiter* and *Kipling*. It was extremely interesting to watch the *Black Swan* being launched, and then gradually fitted out towards completion: and so the weeks of that glorious summer slipped agonisingly by, with the evergrowing knowledge of the certainty of approaching war.

". . . and . . . this country is now at war with Germany."

Those quiet words of Neville Chamberlain came to me in a tobacconist's shop in Scotstoun. On my way to the shipyard I had called in at the shop, and asked if I could listen to the news. When it was over I walked slowly down to the yard, and stood gazing at *Black Swan*, as she sat, mute and half finished, in the fitting-out basin. On that still, grey Sunday morning, she did indeed look like a real swan, asleep on the surface of the water. I pondered for some time what her fate would be.

She certainly looked a grand little ship and able to give a good account of herself. She was a vessel of 2,000 tons and she had six four-inch guns, arranged in pairs on a new type of mounting. Two of these were forward and one aft; they were specially designed for anti-aircraft fire, with an elevation of 80 degrees.

As events turned out this was just as well. She had also a four-barrelled pompom, situated amidships between the masts and therefore directly below the wireless aerials. (When I pointed out to a gunnery expert that this position ensured that the aerials would inevitably be shot away when firing at an aircraft overhead, I was laughed to scorn. Six months later in the chaos of action in Norway this happened time and time again.)

She was fitted with the brand new stabiliser gear, two enormous horizontal fins that could be run out as required under water amidships to stop the ship rolling. In actual practice we did not make use of them a great deal, as when in the "out" position, the noise of the motors controlling them interfered with the working of the Asdic set. The space required to house this gear reduced the boiler space, and the ship's maximum speed was under 20 knots. From the accommodation point of view she was very well fitted out, and it was a great thrill to see her finally finished.

But a ship is not just a matter of steel and iron and wood, she has a personality of her own. That personality comes into being through her Captain, officers and ship's company. In

Captain A. L. Poland, D.S.C. we had as fine a skipper as one could wish for: he had held destroyer command in peacetime, but his most recent appointment was Commander of Chatham Barracks. Correct, a strict disciplinarian but with a keen sense of humour, he was—by reason of the disparity in age between us—very like a father to the rest of us: which, I suppose, is what the Captain of a ship should be.

Lieutenant Jimmy Tennyson, D.S.C., the Pilot, was an ex-Dartmouth type like myself: an amusing messmate, fond of games of every sort, he did his job well and had no inhibitions. Sub-Lieutenant Jack Holmes, the Sub, had been promoted from the Lower Deck: he was very conscientious, though his main job as Correspondence Officer, without the aid of a competent Writer rating, sometimes rather got him down.

Gunner Johnnie Duggan, "Guns", was a typical keen young West Country man: cheerful and loyal, he had his job completely buttoned up. Surgeon-Lieutenant Bob Lander, the Doc, combined reliable professional knowledge with an extensive knowledge of life with a capital "L". Always good-humoured, generally with a ripe story on tap, he was a great asset to the ship. Himself a County rugger player, he was a good Sports Officer.

Anyhow, we all shook down together pretty well in the wardroom, and in January, 1940, the ship commissioned fully.

Deep snow lay everywhere to greet the main body of the crew who arrived, thoroughly miserable, after a typical wartime train journey from Devonport.

Next day we sailed down the Clyde to Greenock where we worked all night—in even deeper snow—ammunitioning ship. After our trials in the Clyde in pretty miserable weather, we sailed for Portland for a three-week work-up. During this time the weather was even worse, and almost everything that could go wrong did so. Still, we were left in peace by the enemy, and gradually achieved some measure of efficiency. With one or two exceptions the ship's company promised very well.

In March, 1940, we sailed up Channel, and joined up with our first northbound convoy as a member of the Rosyth Escort Force. The latter, based on Rosyth, was a mixed collection of destroyers and sloops, whose main duty was to escort the East

Coast convoys from the Forth to the Thames, and back. The majority of these ships were colliers from the Tyne and Tees, whose skippers were sturdy independent types, deeply distrustful of the whole convoy business. They knew the East Coast like the back of their hands, and did not want to be chivvied about like a herd of sheep by young puppies of destroyer Captains.

Escorting these huge convoys—sometimes of fifty ships or more—who sailed in two lines at a depressingly slow speed, was no child's play. Collisions were just as great a menace as was damage by the enemy. This was a thousand times more so at night-time when two convoys, one southbound and the other northbound, had to pass. This invariably occurred with clockwork precision at a corner on the route, when there would be sometimes nearly a hundred ships, all without lights and in darkness, barging past each other in confined waters, with a minefield on one side and sandbanks on the other.

However, *Black Swan* had only done a couple of these trips when she was ordered elsewhere at very short notice. During the first week of April, the word "NORWAY" blazed into prominence out of the gloom of the phoney war.

In the early hours of 8th April, a small British force of mine-laying destroyers laid a minefield off the entrance to West Fiord, the channel to the port of Narvik. This was an attempt to disrupt the German ships carrying ore from that port to Germany. The Norwegian Government were informed, but their indignant protests were swamped by the German invasion of Norway itself the very next day.

By wholesale ruthlessness and clockwork timing the Germans fell upon Norway with troops, ships and troop-carrying aircraft. Although the initial force did not exceed two thousand men, the follow-up from Bremen, Hamburg, Stettin and Danzig consisted of seven divisions. Eight hundred operational aircraft and nearly three hundred troop-carriers descended on the innocent Norwegians. Ten German destroyers arrived up at Narvik, to which port for some days supposedly empty German ore ships had been taking stores and ammunition. Within forty-eight hours the whole of South Norway had been overrun, and the major ports of Oslo, Stavanger, Trondheim and Bergen were in German hands.

Meanwhile at sea there had been several naval actions. The minelaying destroyer, *Glowworm*, temporarily separated from the rest of her force, had attacked and damaged by ramming the cruiser *Hipper* before being herself sunk. The battle-cruiser *Renown* had engaged and damaged the *Gneisenau* at long range in a furious gale and snowstorm. Five "H" Class destroyers had entered Narvik Fiord and, after sinking some enemy merchantships, had fought a fierce engagement with the ten German destroyers previously referred to: both sides suffered heavily, our losses being *Hunter* and *Hardy*.

The next day, the battleship *Warspite* and a flotilla of "Tribal" Class destroyers entered Narvik Fiord, and after an even fiercer engagement, all eight surviving German destroyers were sunk without loss to our force. Meanwhile a British convoy with 4,000 troops had been despatched to the Narvik area, and landed at Harstad on 15th April under the combined leadership of General Mackesy and Admiral Lord Cork. A second and smaller force under General de Wiart had landed at Namsos on the 14th. Several other operations were being hastily planned, and *Black Swan* was amongst the many ships involved.

On Sunday 14th, we had just come in from an East Coast Convoy and were alongside in the pens in Rosyth dockyard with three others of our class, *Flamingo*, *Bittern* and *Auckland*. In the early days of the war, many ships tried to adhere as near as possible to some sort of Sunday routine, and I was on deck making arrangements for a service when the Captain sent for me.

He was standing by his desk with a steely glint in his eye and a pink signal pad in his hand.

"Good morning, Number One, I'm afraid you'll have to cancel any plans that you've made. The balloon's gone up. We're off to Norway."

There followed a day which was a novelty for the *Black Swan* then, but which became only too commonplace as the war went on. A day of humping apparently endless amounts of stores and ammunition; a day of short meal hours and, as it wore on, of even shorter tempers; a day which carried on far into the night, when a hundred Royal Marines suddenly appeared and marched on board, cold and hungry.

All night long we were at it, and then equally suddenly, it was the next day, and in a wild, wet dawn, the *Black Swan* sailed with the three other ships. All three of us were very overloaded; stores were lashed down on the upper decks; the magazines were filled with ammunition for howitzer guns; down on the messdecks the "Royals" sat stolidly grasping their rifles, for there was no room for them to move around.

As we cleared May Island a strong north-easterly wind and an unpleasant swell met us. The scenes down below were beyond description when the coxswain accompanied me on my rounds that night.

"Let's hope it eases down soon, sir," I reported to the Captain a few minutes later. "I don't think either the ship's company or the 'Royals' feel very war-like tonight."

I didn't myself either, but thought it wiser not to say so. Fortunately, during the night a signal ordered the four ships into Cromarty Firth, where we had a few hours to sort ourselves out. It was a perfect sunny spring morning, and I thought of the last time I had been there as a midshipman thirteen years previously. My day-dreams were rudely interrupted by the Captain hailing me.

"Is that our motor-boat going ashore, Number One?"

"Yes, sir—I sent the postman in with the mails."

"That wasn't very bright of you—he'll have told everyone he meets that we're off to Norway."

When we sailed at noon the weather had improved, and the lower deck was cleared for the Captain to inform the ship's company what was happening.

"The object of this expedition," explained the Captain, "is to land the Marines at the port of Andalsnes in Norway, and then to remain there as long as we are required to give them support, particularly against enemy aircraft. More than that I cannot tell you, except that this is called operation 'Primrose'. I am quite sure that whatever happens, it won't be a pansy affair."

The first thrill came on the afternoon of the 16th, as we made our way through a blinding snowstorm to the mouth of Romsdals Fiord. Aircraft reports were received of a force of three enemy destroyers off the coast; in the charthouse I watched the Pilot, with fingers frozen in his wet mittens, plot their position.

"They appear to be heading for the same fiord as we are, sir," he called up the voice-pipe, "and should arrive about the same time. Though God knows," he whispered to me, "if we'll ever find the ruddy entrance in this muck; we had no sights at all on the way across."

The Captain pressed the alarm bell, and the crew ran to action stations, cursing the unfortunate "Royals" who, willy-nilly, blocked every gangway. I climbed up to the director and, as Gunnery Control Officer, ran through the preliminary drill. Then I reported to the Captain, "Main armament ready."

The snowstorm began to ease, and suddenly through the flurries, land appeared before us, a black, rocky coast with the white finger of a solitary lighthouse beckoning us in.

"Thank God," muttered the Pilot, "I'm far more concerned about 'getting into the right hole' than meeting the enemy." He was just grinning at me in smug satisfaction, and bending over the compass to get a bearing, when a series of excited reports rang out.

"Three ships right ahead, sir."

I leapt back into the director.

"Ships in sight on the starboard bow, sir!"

"Alarm starboard; all guns follow director!"

I will not forget that moment. There they were, three enemy ships coming out of the fiord. I gazed with straining eyes through the binoculars in the director sight. On the bridge just below me, the Captain, Officer of the Watch, signalmen and look-outs were doing the same thing. For a matter of seconds there was complete silence, then the Captain lowered his glasses. "They are three of our cruisers," he said calmly. At that moment the leading one started flashing a lamp.

"Challenge correct, sir," called the signalman.

"Make the reply, then," said the Captain. "Relax, every-body." The excitement died down as quickly as it had started, but it left me wondering what would have been the answer if they had been the enemy.

It was now about five o'clock; our force of ships entered the sheltered fiord, and stopped to transfer some written orders from ship to ship by boat. The weather had cleared and it was full moon. It was decided to press on up to Andalsnes (seventy miles inland in a cul-de-sac at the end of Romsdals Fiord) and put the "Royals" and their gear ashore in the dark.

"In the dark" summed up the situation in more ways than one. "I don't wish to appear fussy," I said during a quick supper in the wardroom, "but what we want to know is this— are we going to be greeted by cheers and kisses from Norwegian blondes, or by a hail of gun-fire from invisible Huns? It would make a considerable difference not only to my own peace of mind, but also to my arrangements for putting these chaps ashore on arrival. Does anybody know exactly what the hell is going on?"

But nobody did, and a disjointed signal which was received shortly afterwards to the effect that German submarines might be encountered in the fiords did not help matters.

Led by the *Black Swan*, and with the crews at action stations, the four little ships steamed up the narrow waters. On either side the black rocky heights towered above us, the snowy peaks glistening in the cold moonlight. It really was very exciting, and everyone spoke in subdued tones. At one point we passed under an overhead electric cable stretched right across the fiord, and seemingly only a few feet above the mast.

The tension grew as the ships turned the last corner, and Andalsnes came into view: all eyes scanned the jetty, but there was not a sign of life as the *Black Swan* nosed her way alongside. Then a few figures came running out and took our wires, greetings were exchanged in Norwegian, and everyone breathed again.

The disembarkation took place smoothly, and at three o'clock, *Black Swan* moved off to let another ship take her place. Unfortunately the fiord was too deep to anchor, except in one spot uncomfortably close to the shore, and the ship had to remain under way all night, which involved extra duties for many.

About four I went to bed, worn out like everyone else on board, and it only seemed a few seconds later that I was roused by the sunlight streaming in through the scuttle, and with it the roar of aircraft engines. I ran out on deck and gazed up, blinking in the brilliant sunshine. An aircraft with strange markings was circling the ship, and as I tried to focus my gaze, a man leant out and waved. Then the plane flew away over the hill.

The Sub was on duty in the director. "Norwegian marks, Number One. Lucky I didn't open fire," he called out. "Damn nearly did, though. But that chap will get it in the neck from someone if he goes on like that."

I nodded yawningly, and had a look round. It was a morning of intense beauty. The sun shone down from a blue sky on the calm waters of the fiord and the little town of Andalsnes with its red- and blue-roofed houses, nestling at the end of a long valley under the snow-capped heights. Nothing could have been more peaceful, and nobody guessed that there were only a few hours of peace left.

The morning passed quietly, and by dinner time all traces of the previous days' adventures had been cleaned up. *Bittern* and *Auckland* had pushed off to another port, leaving ourselves and *Flamingo* in the fiord. We were just sitting down to lunch in the wardroom when a messenger knocked on the door.

"There's an aircraft bombin' *Flamingo*, sir," he announced stolidly; he might have reported that it had just started raining.

With a crash of chairs we rose as one man from the table.

"Well for God's sake ring the alarm bells," I shouted. "Don't come all the way down here without doing that."

I pushed past the messenger and streaked up the ladder, but before I could reach the alarm bell push, two heavy explosions rocked the ship from stem to stern. There was no need to press the bell, for the crew were already scrambling to their stations, many of them still chewing a mouthful of dinner.

"Trust the Hun to come in the dinner-hour," remarked the Captain, as he arrived on the bridge. "We shall have to look out for this, Number One."

Within a few minutes another bomber appeared, and the *Black Swan's* guns fired their first shots in anger. Little puffs of grey smoke appeared in the blue sky, gratifyingly close to the target, and the latter flew away out of sight.

When the Check Fire was given, a buzz of excitement spread round the ship. "Even if nothing else happens," said the Sub, "we can at least say we've been in action now." He was to remember that remark during the next few days.

The next few days—it seems like an impossible dream when

I look back on it. From dawn to dusk the *Black Swan* steamed round the confined waters of the fiord, sidestepping the bombs, and firing away like an angry bee. The expression, "Buzzing about like a bee in a lavatory," kept occurring to me.

At first it was quite exciting. The bombs always managed to fall well clear, and no harm was done. It seemed more like a game than anything serious, and on the second morning I was quite sure we had shot at least one aircraft down, if not two.

But then things began to change; the same afternoon one stick of bombs fell mighty close, and, due to an error on my part, the guns failed to open fire and the plane flew away unscathed. Not anticipating such an extensive period of firing, we had blazed away merrily even at extreme ranges, and it became increasingly clear that we were going to run short of ammunition.

The long periods of being closed up at action stations began to tell on many of the men, particularly those cooped up down below, who had not much idea of what was going on except for the fact that someone was slinging bombs at them. I realised that well enough, but when I tried relaxing to any extent during daylight hours, the harsh clanging of the alarm bell recalling us to our stations had an even worse effect on everyone's nerves.

It began to dawn on everyone that the whole Norwegian campaign was not going as well as might be expected. We heard the *Bittern* had been hit after intense bombing and sunk in a neighbouring fiord, and news of other losses at sea were received. When we berthed alongside occasionally, the local Norwegians had nothing to tell but tales of disaster, and the Captain, who was also Senior Naval Officer present, had to spend much of his time out of the ship dealing with problems ashore which daily grew more and more complex. The scarcity of interpreters did not help; there were two, one of whom was a doctor, in the Naval H.Q. staff of about twenty men now left at Andalsnes. On the third morning the Doc came into my cabin, pale and red-eyed from lack of sleep.

"Look, Number One, I must have someone to help me with these cyphers—I just can't compete."

The signal situation was getting out of hand. Streams of messages flowed in day and night in a certain cypher designated as "Only to be handled by an officer." The Doctor normally did this, assisted by any officer off watch. But we were spending most of the day at action stations, and in the brief spells between banging away at the Hun, we wanted a spot of rest.

"Look at this lot," said the Doc, pointing to a tray of signals. "I haven't touched that yet. Some of them are over twenty-four hours old—half are out of date anyhow."

Events were moving so fast ashore on the overall picture that by the time any signal had been written out, encyphered and transmitted, the situation had completely changed. Time and again, as I had foreseen six months earlier, the wireless aerials were shot away by the over-enthusiastic pompom crew.

Disregarding regulations, I got some ratings in to help the Doctor, and the officers lent a hand whenever possible. But we were nearly driven mad by it. Not only nearly mad, but very depressed. For it did not need much intelligence to see from the signals that we *did* decypher, that the campaign was rapidly getting out of hand.

"Half these people haven't the foggiest idea what's going on," I said angrily, after we had spent ages over one particularly fatuous signal, "the whole situation's absolutely——"

"—arse over heels," agreed the Doc, with that delicacy of phrase for which he was so famous.

Secretly I was beginning to wonder how much longer our own luck would hold out. The near misses were getting much nearer; one bomb, which missed the stem by a few feet, miraculously did not explode. I remember noticing it with a curiously detached view, and not being unduly worried.

The ship's company stood up well under the strain. The Chief Gunner's Mate, Petty Officer Bullock, and whose frame matched his name, was a tower of strength: the Chief Boat-swain's Mate, a typical West Country stalwart, was another one out of the Chiefs and Petty Officers who showed a high standard of cheerful discipline.

"Can I lower the boats this afternoon, sir?" asked the C.B.M.—we were lying alongside Andalsnes at the time, and things had eased off somewhat. "What for?" I asked, "want to row home?"

"No, sir—to pick up all them fish. Enough to give the 'ole ship's company a fry tonight."

So away went the whaler and motor boat to return in due course with a fine collection. While they were unloading, the cruiser *Carlisle* came up the fiord and started flashing at us. In a few minutes—

"First Lootenant, sir," bawled one of our signalmen, "Signal from *Carlisle*. 'Send boat for Admiral forthwith'."

But the boat was still full of codfish: our P.O. steward was selecting one or two with the air of a connoisseur.

"Brace up, Davies," I called out, as I saw the *Carlisle* flashing angrily, and in fact, I read the signal.

"What—is—the—delay?—send—boat—at—once."

"All right," I said crossly, "go over now."

The Admiral gave me a pretty frosty look when he came ashore: still, it was worth it. You don't often see an Admiral in a small boat surrounded by dead cod! He had hardly stepped ashore when the *Carlisle* started flashing again.

"From—which—direction—and—how—do—the—air—attacks—develop?"

Before we could reply an enemy aircraft whizzed over the top of the fiord, dropped two bombs, luckily wide of the mark, and zoomed away. When the splashes had subsided, we replied:

"Like—that."

On the evening of the 21st we had orders to return to Scapa. The trip across was uneventful, and of course we all wanted to write home and tell our families what heroes we had been. Some of the crew certainly possessed remarkable powers of imagination. One letter I had to read as Censor contained a lurid description of a party with a Norwegian blonde. I knew for certain that the writer had never put foot ashore!

CHAPTER II

THE GREAT ESCAPE

A T SCAPA we heard how the Norwegian Campaign was
progressing: the news was far from good. Between the
17th April and 23rd the situation had developed as
follows.

In the far north at Narvik there was a complete standstill.
Admiral Lord Cork was eager to attack Narvik with the force
then based at Harstad, but General Mackesy would not agree:
so the precious days slipped by, and the Germans in Narvik
had time to re-organise their defences.

In Central Norway, the Allies decided to try and regain
Trondheim. A direct assault from seaward—operation "Ham-
mer"—by ships of the Home Fleet, supported by the R.A.F.,
was planned on the 17th to take place on the 22nd.

But almost immediately there was opposition by the Chiefs
of Staff, who reckoned the plan was too risky, and so the
seaward attack was cancelled. The alternative was a landward
"pincer" attack by the two military forces already landed at
Namsos, to the northward, and at Andalsnes, to the southward.
This was agreed upon, and large numbers of troops were
thereupon switched to Namsos and Andalsnes. In the
meantime, it was decided that an attack on Narvik must be
postponed.

The "pincer" attack on Trondheim was a complete failure.
From Namsos, General de Wiart set off southwards down the
road, and a brigade of his troops reached Verdal, only fifty
miles from Trondheim at the head of the fiord. But the
Germans immediately sent a much stronger force by sea from
Trondheim, and after heavy fighting, the British suffered considerable losses and were forced to retreat in intolerable snow
conditions back to Namsos; here they were bombed continuously in daylight hours.

A very similar fate meanwhile befell the southern arm of the "pincer" the mixed force which had set off from Andalsnes to Dombas and Lillehammer. Here Brigadier Morgan's Infantry, plus the original landing party of Marines, had joined the Norwegian C.-in-C., General Ruge, with a remnant of his forces; these were being engaged by three divisions of Germans driving northward along the road and railway from Oslo. The situation from the Allied point of view was desperate, and reinforcements were hurried to Andalsnes, and thence along the railway towards Dombas to try and stem the oncoming Germans. The reinforcements under General Paget arrived only in time to fight a rearguard action.

After the briefest of spells in Scapa, long enough only to refuel and re-ammunition, the *Black Swan* had orders to return to Andalsnes. The retention of this little port was clearly of vital importance to the Allies. Just before sailing there occurred an error of judgment on my part which I have always since regretted. A signal was received asking us to take a Press photographer with us. The Captain said "No", but I felt that if I had pressed the point he would have changed his mind. That photographer would have certainly had some shots in a thousand had he come along!

Our trip across the North Sea was without incident, but gloom spread over all on board on the afternoon of the 24th as we entered the fiord. The rocky heights seemed to close down on the little ship in the most ominous manner, producing a rat in a trap atmosphere. A heavy pall of smoke hung over Andalsnes, which had been badly damaged by German bombers, who now came and went almost at their leisure. The First Lieutenant of the sloop we were relieving came aboard to see me.

"I'll tell you straight away, old boy, that the situation is pretty punk," he said, "and I think we may have to pack our bags and 'ammicks before very long. Nobody knows what the hell's happening inland, and in the air the Hun comes and goes as he pleases. We spent the last three days banging away from morning till night at these baskets, who come zipping over the top of the hill, let go their loads and buzz off. I think we may have winged a few, but I haven't seen any bite the dust, and we've had some pretty narrow squeaks. Half the town's been blown to hell, and the locals spend their time asking us for food. Apart from all that, the situation's fine."

The next few days, the 25th, 26th and 27th, were a replica of the first visit, but the tempo of the attack increased. The Germans seemed determined to get rid of the *Black Swan* at all costs: some of the dive-bombing attacks were carried out with great bravery. I remember one fellow coming straight at the director regardless of our fire. Through my binoculars I could see popples of flame along his wings.

"We've hit him anyhow," I shouted to the layer beside me. It was only when bullets whined past us and I saw splinters of steel chipped out of the upper-works and mast that I realised the flames came from his own cannon.

At least two attackers were shot down on the first afternoon. I saw them crash vertically into the sides of the fiord like plummetting pheasants. But there was no time for congratulations all round before the next attackers appeared, and the situation was "just one damn thing after another". We had some very near misses, and the ship's side and upper works were riddled with splinter holes. My cabin was one of many places to be drilled clean as a whistle through desk, chair and bulkhead.

"I've got a better one," remarked the Doc, "a cut right across the front of my burberry, like a razor slash. I'll wear it in Bessie's Bar at the North-British, and give that red-head a thrill. Of course," he added, "she need never know it was on a hook in my cabin at the time."

The thought occurred to me that we would be damn lucky to see the inside of *any* bar again, let alone the red-head in Bessie's; but before I could say so, the alarm bells went, and two minutes later the bridge personnel were soused with spray as a stick of bombs straddled us. Once again our luck held, and no real damage resulted.

"Well, I suppose it's one way of spending Saturday afternoon," remarked the Pilot mopping his face, "but personally I'd rather be playing golf."

"This time last year I was at Wembley givin' Pompey a chuck-up," grinned one of the signalmen. "Look out, sir, here's another of the swine—port beam, coming in low!"

So the day wore on, and as darkness fell we returned

alongside the jetty. Although no aircraft had been seen to come down, I felt sure that some had been hit. We had fired over 300 rounds of 4-inch, and many more of pompom. The upper deck was stacked with the brass empties, and the reek of cordite was everywhere. Fortunately a cruiser had arrived during the day, and left 400 rounds for us before proceeding elsewhere. Wearily, but in high spirits, the sailors carried them on board in the darkness.

I remember the Captain's words as we stood on the upper deck: "Nobody will ever really fathom the British matelot," he said. "Possibly it is best that way. In times of peace and plenty they will have a most awful moan over something apparently quite trivial, yet when the situation's awful they will always rise to the occasion. The worse it is, the better they are. Look at these chaps now. Tired as hell, bombed to blazes all day, and to listen to them, one might imagine that they were in Queen Street, Pompey, on a Saturday might."

Snatches of conversation drifted up from the men working in the ammunition lighter. "'Ere y'ar, Nobby, take this one to bed wiv yer ternight."—"Cheer up, Ginger, only another five tharsand."—"Now then, Collins, get some of yer ruddy torpedoes ready."

I turned away grinning, and half-collided with the Sub. The latter was breathless with excitement. "I say, Number One, there's an Army bloke just come aboard who says we shot at least three down this afternoon. He saw them crash, and sent some of his chaps out, and they've picked up seven Germans. They're here now on the jetty."

It was quite true, and the news spread quickly round the ship. "Put them down in the lighter now, sir, to give us an 'and with this ammo," suggested the Gunner's mate, laughing.

"I'd like to take them to sea with us tomorrow," I replied, "that would shake them." Already half the ship's company were on the jetty staring like children at the zoo at the little group of airmen. It was a curious situation, and somehow rather embarrassing. I was quite glad when the Army officer took them off under guard, after telling us he hoped there would be more to collect next day. Through the darkness there soon appeared streaks of light; and so Sunday, 28th April dawned.

Black Swan left the jetty at daylight, and about 9.30 the first attack was made. For over an hour we fired almost continually, and had some miraculous escapes. Then there was a lull, and the fiord was bathed in sunshine, quiet and still. It was a Sunday morning, and the whole business that we were engaged in seemed quite fantastic.

"Pass the word," I shouted down the voicepipe from my seat in the gun director, "that there will be no Divisions[1] this morning."

It was not a terribly funny joke, but it produced roars of laughter in the transmitting station, and I could hear the faint echoes from each gun as the message reached them. I took my tin helmet off and mopped my brow; my head was aching with the noise and the effort of concentrating on the drill. I glanced at my watch. It was 10.45. Time for church at home, I thought.

Just about now the family would be arriving at the gate; the car would be parked at the usual place up against the old grey stone wall, and they would walk slowly up the path to the porch. On either side there would be a yellow blaze of daffodils in the churchyard, and from a blue sky overhead, the sun. . . .

"Right overhead, sir, in the sun—two of 'em." The director layer's voice was hoarse as he tapped my sleeve. I came back to reality with a start.

"Aircraft in sight, bearing red nine zero, all guns follow director, stand by for a run. . . ."

My God, I thought, I hope they pray hard for us today.

The bombs came down. . . .

It was just after three o'clock that it happened. It became increasingly obvious that our luck could not hold out much longer. All the rounds so laboriously taken inboard the night before had been expended, and although at least three more aircraft had been brought down, it did not seem to worry the enemy.

We had entered a small inlet with the hope of escaping detection, when a dive-bomber swung over the heights and screamed down on our starboard beam. The next few seconds seemed a hundred years. Vaguely I heard the Captain's order on the bridge.

[1] i.e. Church Parade.

"Full ahead together, hard-a-starboard!"

"Barrage short, commence, commence, commence!"

For the hundredth time I shouted down the voicepipe to the transmitting station. "Open fire, pompom!"

In the brilliant sunlight I could see the pilot clearly as the bomb was released at masthead height; then the aircraft zoomed away, surrounded by tracer bullets. I looked aft, and my heart went cold. I gained a split-second impression of Guns on duty at the after mounting, gazing open-mouthed up at the descending horror, then I saw it hit the quarter-deck just below him. A little puff of smoke went up from the wooden deck, and that was all.

"Good God!"

The layer and I spoke as one man. We gazed at each other in amazement; then the ship shook as a muffled explosion sounded astern. I looked aft again. The ship was still whole. I saw Guns pick himself up, and run down the ladder below decks where the bomb had disappeared. Then he came up on deck, hurried up to the bridge, and I heard him reporting to the Captain.

"It's almost unbelievable, sir. It's gone right through the wardroom, through the corner of the after fresh-water tank into the after magazine, and out of the bottom of the ship. The explosion must have been underwater."

"Not only that, sir," added Chiefee a few minutes later, "but it's gone out between the propellor shafts without touching either of them."

It was, indeed, one of the most miraculous escapes any ship ever had: and, in addition to my immediate reaction of complete relief, I can remember thinking to myself—"Well, we're quite O.K. now: they've hit us once—they won't try again." Which just shows what a fool I was: for within a few minutes of our being hit, we were attacked again. We fired back rather wildly, and luckily the bombs fell clear.

When I had a chance, I nipped down aft to see the damage. Nobody had been killed, but the three men in the magazine were badly wounded. One was the canteen manager: the bomb had actually gone between him and another rating as they stood only a few feet apart, putting shells into the hoist. In the wardroom the shipwright and his staff had plugged the hole in the hull, but not before the wardroom had been flooded to a depth of a foot. The whole place was a frightful mess, for the bomb had in fact gone through the table, which had splintered all over the place. Curiously enough, the wireless was intact and still switched on; we listened more or less in a dream to the 4 o'clock news:

"The situation in Norway," came the smooth punctilious voice of the announcer, "is somewhat confused . . ."

"You're —— well right there, mate!" said the shipwright.

The outlook was grim. Only seventeen rounds of 4-inch ammunition remained in the whole of the ship for the main armament, and there was no prospect of any more anywhere at hand. Fortunately the attacks eased off, and by dark we were back at Andalsnes without further incident.

"Well, it's no use staying here with a crippled ship and no ammunition," said the Captain. "I've signalled the Admiralty we are leaving for Scapa tonight, as soon as we can collect anyone who wants to come. The town's had an awful bashing this afternoon, and the orders have gone out to evacuate the place."

It was tragic to see the little wooden houses burning away: some had tipped up sideways, and lay like dolls' houses upset in anger by a naughty child. By this time we were all feeling the strain a bit.

"I reckon the chaps need an extra spot of rum, Number One," said the Doc, and I nodded assent without really thinking twice about it. I was so tired I could hardly think, anyhow; moreover it had just started to snow which did not help matters much. An hour or so later, some of us were in the Captain's cabin (for the wardroom was untenable) wrestling with a signal, when there was a knock on the door and his personal attendant, Leading Steward Grey entered. The latter combined the qualities of a very useful outside-left with those of a first-class steward. On this occasion, anyhow, he was solemnly carrying two tots of rum on a tray, which he offered to the Capain in his most Jeeves-like manner.

"What the devil's this?" asked the Captain.

"Splice the mainbrace, sir. First Lieutenant's orders," replied his steward, blandly.

The Captain looked at me in amazement. "What have you been doing, Number One?"

I just yammered in reply. Only then did I realise that Doc must have taken my nod seriously, and told the Coxswain to go ahead with the extra rum issue. This was, in fact, the case. I must be one of the few officers in the Service who have ever ordered Splice the Main-brace.

The Captain was pretty angry about it. However the signal we were decyphering, fortunately for me, was of greater moment than a few pints of rum. It was a long signal, using the most flowery and verbose phrases, about embarking King Haakon of Norway and taking him to England.

We realised then that things were even grimmer ashore than they were with us. Since returning to Andalsnes, we had not had much chance to keep in touch with the overall picture, as we had spent most of the time dodging round the fiords being bombed. And that pastime (as Dr. Johnson remarked of the man about to be hanged in a fortnight) "concentrates the mind wonderfully."

Anyhow a constant stream of individuals of every type crowded on board—Army, Air Force, Norwegians, Frenchmen and so on. We heard that the Germans were advancing up the railway from Dombas not very far away. I wondered what had happened to all the Marines that we had put ashore only two weeks before.

As soon as possible, therefore, after darkness fell, we shoved off from the jetty, and prepared to leave for Scapa. Then occurred a really exasperating incident. The Senior Officer ashore advised us not to leave before he had given us an important message. A signalman was sent ashore to get it, but in the general chaos, with half the town on fire, he could not find the British Naval Headquarters. This had been shifted from one place to another, and it was not the signalman's fault that we were delayed.

On board, in an agony of mind, we awaited the return of the messenger. There was a seventy-mile land-locked gauntlet to run before the open sea was reached, and we hoped to be well clear before daylight, when we knew the bombing would start again. Frantic with impatience, we watched the precious hours of darkness slip by. It was like one of those ghastly nightmares when you are trying to run from some unknown horror and your legs will not move.

At long last the boat bringing the signalman back was seen returning through the darkness. The ship was moving ahead before the boat was hoisted up clear of the water, but that was well after midnight, and a blinding snowstorm did not make life any easier. Dawn found us only half-way down the fiord waiting for the inevitable attack, and with only seventeen rounds of ammunition left to meet it.

"Don't open fire unless absolutely necessary, Number One," the Captain ordered. "With a spot of luck we may not be sighted."

There was an agonising moment when two Heinkels flew directly overhead, but no attack was made. At the mouth of the fiord we met H.M.S. *Fleetwood*, who had been ordered to relieve us, and we all breathed a sigh of relief.

"What has happened?" came a signal. "Can we help?"

The Captain had not lost his sense of humour. "Lost a few tail feathers, and got no more shells," was the reply.

"Good luck," she answered.

"Same to you; you'll need it," we flashed back, and very aptly, too, for shortly afterwards bombs were seen bursting around them.

Our trip across the North Sea was no picnic, with the ship holed aft and two large compartments flooded—the magazine and the fresh-water tank—and we all felt a bit uneasy. After two days we steamed slowly into Scapa Flow; vile weather for the last twelve hours had made the trip even more hazardous. Darkness was falling as we made for our buoy in Gutter Sound, and I saw the Captain heave a sigh of relief as he gave the order to Ring off Main Engines. Then he stumped slowly down the ladder, grey with fatigue.

I remember very clearly also going aft to my cabin, and slumping down on my bunk, physically exhausted, angry at the damage to our little ship, and thoroughly depressed at the failure of the campaign.

For by then it was quite obvious that we would have to abandon the campaign, and so it turned out. The remnants of the force that had set out from Andalsnes were evacuated from that port on 1st May. Two days later the other party of troops from Namsos were evacuated, and when their convoy was heavily attacked in the North Sea, two destroyers—the French *Bison* and H.M.S. *Afridi*—were sunk.

Although in the far north, a combined assault eventually captured Narvik on 28th May, ten days later they were obliged to withdraw to concentrate all efforts in France and at home. During the withdrawal we suffered considerable losses, the carrier *Glorious* with 1,500 men, destroyers *Ardent* and *Acasta*, the troopship *Orama* and other ships. Luckily the King of Norway and his Ministers were taken safely from Tromso to England in the *Devonshire*.

So ended the Norway Campaign; a failure due to vacillation and divided command at high levels, lack of air support for ships and men, and far too much signal traffic during the campaign.

But curiously enough, to me as a mere individual that is not the way I look at it today: and the memory I have now is of a grand crowd of shipmates, who shared an astonishing adventure, shot down several of their attackers, and brought their damaged ship home safely to fight another day.

Maybe it was not a complete failure after all.

PART TWO

THE EAST COAST CONVOYS

Chapter III

A SECOND BUMP

WE HAD hardly poked our nose inside the boom at Scapa, before signals started pouring in: but they were rather shorter than those which we had struggled with in Norway, and the first one to greet us was the briefest of the lot. It read:

"*Black Swan* from C.-in-C.
Well done."

In addition to the above—and possibly in the opinion of some, more important—the magic word "Leave" was being buzzed about the ship.

In the comparative peace of Scapa Flow, a careful study of the damage we had received at Andalsnes revealed what a really miraculous escape we had had. The bomb had hit the quarterdeck on the one particular spot where the deck was double strengthened to take minelaying rails. Yet it had penetrated straight through this into the wardroom, through the wardroom table and deck into the top corner of the fresh-water tank; thence through a vertical bulkhead into the after four-inch magazine, which was still full of ammunition! There, in its downward flight, the bomb had actually passed between two men standing an arm's length apart as they put 4-inch shells into the ammunition hoist, and then it went straight out of the bottom of the ship, finally exploding underwater.

Not only that, but with the ship under way and the helm hard over so that the stern was swinging to port, the bomb had chosen to pass clean through the bottom of the ship between the two propellor shafts, neither of them being affected. The summing-up then, was that this 450 kg. bomb penetrated four separate thicknesses of steel (i.e. three decks and a bulkhead), passed through a magazine half full of 4-inch ammunition and finally made its exit, still unexploded, from the ship in a neat hole between the two propellor shafts, which at that particular point were about fifteen feet apart. And if all that isn't a miracle, then God knows what is!

At the time it happened in the heat of action, I do not think it dawned on us how lucky we had been. It was only in the cold light of reckoning that the realisation came to us. However, we had made our mark on the Luftwaffe, too. A careful analysis, including neutral reports, showed that *Black Swan* had shot down at least seven aircraft, with another five probables. Norwegians and our own troops near Andalsnes had rounded up a score of airmen prisoners. We had fired nearly 3,000 rounds four-inch, 8,000 rounds of pompom, and we lost count of the smaller stuff. I remember seeing three aircraft come down on land—a very satisfying feeling.

It was agreed that we should be repaired at Falmouth— just about as far away from Scapa Flow as could be imagined. However, with a West Country crew, the prospect had many compensations. So after rather a shaky trip down the West Coast of Scotland and through the Irish Sea we steamed safely into Falmouth. The war had hardly touched Cornwall; the collapse of France was unthinkable and the weather was perfect. Each watch had ten days' leave, and it fell to me to remain on board for the first period. We soon made many friends ashore and had a very enjoyable time. One Sunday afternoon a mixed party of us went for a sailing picnic in the whaler. We fetched up at the little village of St. Mawes, and landed at a small hotel for tea. We lolled in the sunshine laughing and joking on the verandah, while an elderly waiter in spotless tails set out a wonderful spread—Cornish cream, strawberry jam, cakes and so on. I happened to glance at my watch and saw it was half-past three.

"Exactly two weeks ago today," I remarked, sipping my tea in idle luxury, "we were dodging round a Norwegian fiord, being bombed to hell, with the stern of the ship half flooded, and no ammunition left."

When I went home on leave, conditions in the Lake District were equally peaceful. My recent adventures seemed even more like a dream than ever. Returning to the ship at the end of May, the news from the Continent was very bad. The invasion of Holland and Belgium had begun. I discussed the situation with a stranger in the train.

"It's the French I'm worried about," he said. "I think they will surrender."

"The French surrender?" I said in horror. The idea had never entered my head: which just showed how much I knew about the war. The invasion of the Low Countries had started before *Black Swan's* repairs were completed. Security measures were brought into force even in Falmouth; one of the rules was that the shipyard gates were to be closed between midnight and dawn. Nobody was allowed to enter or leave during that period, and thereby hangs a tale.

Two nights before we were due to sail, several of us went to a party given by a very charming lady, Susie Vaughan, at her lovely house, Trevissome, outside Falmouth. There was no question of returning aboard by midnight, so we stayed and danced the whole night through. It was a perfect evening, a really happy "Midsummer Night's Dream".

We returned aboard just in time to carry straight on with the normal day's work. But breakfast with the Captain in his cabin—for the wardroom was being painted—was a real ordeal trying to keep our eyes open. We did not want him to know we had been ashore all night. At lunch time, however, the secret somehow or other came out. The Captain roared with laughter.

"Why the devil didn't you let me know at breakfast?" he said, "I'd have given you all a horse's neck!"

Black Swan left Falmouth and sailed to Devonport to re-ammunition: here a slightly awkward situation arose. For, being a West Country crew, most of the men had their wives and families in that port. But it was the time of Dunkirk and no leave could be given. We ammunitioned as fast as we could, lying at a buoy in midharbour with a crowd of wives and sweethearts gazing forlornly from the beach. On completion, we sailed at high speed to take part in the evacuation from France, but the operation was over by then, so we returned to Rosyth.

Rosyth at this time (June, 1940) was in a very curious state. Buzzes and rumours of all sorts filled the air, and the impending invasion was the main topic of conversation: but here again there were two vastly different bodies of opinion.

Those of us who had been in action, especially the destroyer crews just returned from Dunkirk, and who were employed in continuous service in the ever-increasingly strenuous East Coast convoys, had a very different outlook on life from our opposite numbers in status quo at Rosyth: the latter—including also large numbers of the dockyard and civilians—were inclined to take the typically British, casual, "it-won't-happen-here-anyhow" attitude. This outlook was aided by Rosyth's geographical position far removed from the Low Countries, and also by the fact that there had been practically no air raids in the vicinity.

This fact, for which we were all devoutly thankful, always puzzled me considerably. The Forth Bridge and the huge Naval dockyard were tempting targets: damage to either would have caused enormous inconvenience. But except for one daylight raid early in the war, visitations from enemy aircraft were few and far between. There was, of course, a vast anti-aircraft organisation in force day and night. One of the duties for the Escort Force was known as Duty "A". This involved one destroyer on guard at the convoy anchorage at Methil, halfway down the Firth: nothing happened for a long time, then one night a single aircraft flew in, and torpedoed the sloop *Pelican* who was at anchor. The torpedo hit right aft: by a monumental stroke of luck there were very few casualties, but the whole stern of the ship was bent bodily upwards, exactly like the tilted-up tail of a real duck.

But the bombing of London and South of England ports began to have a serious effect on the morale of ship's crews, as no doubt Hitler hoped it would. Nearly all of *Black Swan's* crew had their homes down in the South and West: and I sensed a feeling of uneasiness among the men. The list of Requests for Compassionate Leave got longer and longer: here again was another problem.

Dealing with such requests was very difficult: much as I sympathised with each request from the personal point of view, I had to steel myself to be hard-hearted from the national point of view. A man's absence from his ship, and particularly a key rating, meant a loss of efficiency which we could not afford just then. The ship had to come first and foremost. Many of the men, and indeed millions of the population, had no idea of the frightful danger that the nation was in at that time. Compassionate leave could just not be given except in the most urgent circumstances.

The question of local leave was also a tricky one. Even when in harbour for a day or so between convoys, the ships were at comparatively short notice for steam in case the balloon went up. It was essential to grant shore leave, and a somewhat unusual scheme was evolved, whereby leave was granted from 1 p.m. to 5 p.m. and then from 7 till 11. The idea like many others was excellent in theory, but vastly different in practice.

It was almost impossible to arrange any games, transport to Dumfermline—the only sizeable town within striking distance —was hopelessly overcrowded, and the dockyard canteen was the main rendezvous for libertymen. The majority of the ship's company behaved themselves admirably, but there was always the odd individual who overdid things, and caused trouble.

From the officer's point of view, the Club up the hill outside the dockyard was a great boon: there were tennis courts and a squash court, billiards, and, of course, a chance to meet feminine company. Cocktail parties went on as usual on board ship, but they were apt to be interrupted by an emergency signal ordering the ship to sea, and occasionally by the air raid siren.

One of the few air raids that did take place occurred one night during *Black Swan's* boiler clean in July: however, no great damage was done.

A rather happier incident took place the very next day. My wife, accompanied by her brother and his wife, was staying in a small hotel in Inverkeithing, and the four of us planned to play tennis that afternoon. I was rather late getting away from the ship.

"Anything wrong?" I was asked on arrival at the hotel.

"Not exactly," was my reply, "I've just heard I've got a D.S.C."

When we eventually played tennis, it was an exhilarating game, if not of a very high standard.

A list of awards for some of us in *Black Swan*, following on our Norway adventure, had arrived in the ship that forenoon. Captain Poland, who had gained a well-deserved D.S.O., subsequently invited the four of us to a dinner party on board. It was a very pleasant evening during what I always consider the darkest spell of the war. A spell when that terrible cloud of uncertainty, tension, and even a suspicion of fear hung over us all.

And here let me record, with a glow of pride that fills me even now fifteen years afterwards, two of the finest examples of leadership I have ever met. The first was in the wardroom of the sloop H.M.S. *Egret*, commanded by Captain D. P. (Dippy) Evans. The *Egret* was alongside at Rosyth on that fateful day in late June when the French Government capitulated. There was a crowd of us young officers in the *Egret's* wardroom having a pre-lunch drink, when the grim news came through on the wireless. When the announcement finished there was dead silence, and instinctively, we all turned to the Captain.

Dippy looked round at us with his infectious smile.

"That's all right, chaps," he said quietly. "We'll whack 'em alone. We did it before, we'll do it again. Don't worry."

The second incident was one of a more national character. It has been truly said that Sir Winston Churchill wrote his own epitaph in that single phrase "We will never surrender."

On the day of that famous broadcast some of us were sitting in the wardroom of the *Black Swan*. We were worn out after an exacting convoy, gloomy, and in fact—in naval parlance—thoroughly "chokker".

Someone turned on the wireless for the Prime Minister's broadcast, and as his message came through at once a change stole over us. A chuckle here, a surreptitious smile exchanged, a murmured comment of approval—we are not a demonstrative race on the whole, and naval officers perhaps least of all. Gradually our spirits rose, and I have no doubt that the same thing was happening in a million homes or more. Indeed it might be no exaggeration to say that that was one of the most dramatic moments in the life of the whole nation.

Be that as it may, never to my dying day shall I forget how as one man we rose to our feet with a shout, punching each other playfully on the shoulders, all gloom forgotten and confidence completely restored, when from the wireless on the bulkhead came that bulldog growl:

"We will never surrender."

I hope Hitler was listening too: and if so, doubtless his reactions were somewhat different. But I always think how furious he must have been for nearly four years after that speech, as he gazed so enviously across the Straits of Dover. So near and yet so far.

I am second to none in my admiration for all the other Services, and especially the R.A.F., in that "finest hour" of 1940. But let nobody forget that although Hitler advanced triumphantly, like another tyrant over a hundred years before, all those many miles across Europe towards his main enemy, he was defeated by the last twenty-two of them.

Because the last twenty-two miles were salt water, and the Navy was ready there waiting for him. In the North Sea, in the Straits of Dover, and in the English Channel. Bruised and a bit breathless, maybe, after Dunkirk—but still there.

In the meantime, we had to get on with our work—the East Coast convoys; the question of coastal traffic in the North Sea is very important. In peacetime nearly all the coal for industrial purposes in the South of England is brought by sea in a varied collection of colliers from Tyne and Tees down to the Thames estuary.

In wartime, naturally these ships had to sail in convoy both southward when fully laden, and northward when in ballast. Many other types of ships sailed in the convoy, too, but the majority were colliers. So for the whole war there was a kind of non-stop nautical train service up and down the East Coast, with ships joining and leaving at the various intermediate ports like coaches being shunted off a train. This coastal convoy was going on all round the British Isles, of course, but the section that came in for the worst hammering both from the weather and the enemy, was undoubtedly that between the Forth and the Thames.

In all I spent nearly three years with the East Coast convoys, and came to know the drill pretty well by the end of that time. It was a most worthwhile job in every way, and nearly every convoy was packed with incident, particularly for the commanding officers of the escorts, who had tremendous responsibilities to shoulder.

At the same time no actual trip lasted more than three days; at Rosyth the escorts were assured of a berth alongside, and from 1941 onwards, a regular boiler clean with four days leave a month. In 1940, however, matters were very different. After Dunkirk there were few escorts available, and the threat of invasion hung over all. At times a convoy of fifty ships would have one destroyer as its escort. As the ships proceeded in two columns only, a convoy of this size would stretch about ten miles. It was impossible for a single escort to keep an eye on the whole convoy. Quite often the rear ships were attacked by air or mined, and the escort in the van knew nothing about it. Still, "by guess and by God" the convoys went on running.

For navigational purposes the convoy proceeded down a set route, marked by light buoys about every five miles. This route was swept as frequently as possible by our minesweepers, and became known as the Tramlines. It was only a few hundred yards wide and not completely foolproof. In spite of the most skilled and strenuous work by minesweepers, many ships were sunk by mines even on the prescribed route. To wander off the Tramlines was just asking for trouble—unfortunately many ships did so, and got it. Air attacks on the convoy were an almost daily occurrence. With the R.A.F. holding the fort over the South coast, there were no fighters available for regular escort of East coast convoys. When they did arrive they scored several successes.

On July 1st, 1940, we were off the Tees with a southbound convoy about six o'clock in the morning, when we sighted an unusual aircraft hovering round. It was a white seaplane with red crosses painted on its fuselage, and while we were wondering whether to open fire or not, the question was settled for us by a couple of Spitfires, who zoomed up from nowhere and shot the machine down into the sea. It did not sink immediately, and four men climbed out into a rubber dinghy. We stopped, and I went over in the whaler to investigate. The machine was a Heinkel 115, and I climbed on board and retrieved as much as I could in the way of maps and papers, before it sank.

The crew were highly indignant at being shot down. They explained they were an unarmed rescue plane and looking for any German pilots who had been shot down. Their long cock-and-bull story could, of course, be explained in one word . . . Reconnaissance. We landed them at Middlesbrough, and rejoined the convoy. A few hours later a Heinkel III was shot down over the convoy and landed in the sea near *Black Swan*. Away I went in the whaler again; we fished three Germans out of the sea, and carried out a somewhat amateur interrogation,

The pilot of the machine was a typically Nazi fellow, boastful and arrogant. His rantings were perhaps accentuated by the half tumblerful of brandy that I gave him—with a purpose—in my cabin.

"You have picked me up. I am your prisoner," he said scornfully. "What does it matter? In a few weeks our armies will be in England and the war will be over."

I ventured to express a different opinion.

"Bah," replied the German, "What have you got to stop us? Nothing! Why, in Berlin now they are getting ready for the victory parade!"

As the summer wore on, the Battle of Britain increased in intensity. Coming into the Thames estuary, we used to watch the aerial combats overhead in those wonderful summer days, when the cloudless blue sky was criss-crossed with white vapour trails of the dog-fights overhead.

One memory I will always treasure to the end of my life. A squadron of German bombers was sighted to the eastward flying in perfect formation, about sixty in all, steadily and unharmed towards London. We opened fire but they sailed relentlessly on, disdainful of the puffs of the shells. Nothing, it seemed, could stop them.

Suddenly the Captain rang the Cease Fire bell. From out of the west three of our fighters hurled themselves head on towards the enemy. For a few seconds we watched, breathless, to see who would give way. Then the Germans broke formation as our three fighters sailed into their midst, and the usual schemozzle started. As we watched, one of the fighters hurtled downwards: a parachute opened and fluttered down into the estuary half a mile ahead. We soon had the pilot safely on board: he was quite unhurt and eager to be back in the fray.

The Germans did not neglect the convoys either. One blazing hot September afternoon we were northbound with a convoy off Lowestoft. Nothing had happened for some hours, and undoubtedly a slight air of drowsiness had affected those even on watch. On deck the hands off watch lay sleeping in the sunshine. Suddenly with an appalling succession of "woomfs", *Black Swan* was completely straddled by four bombs, two bursting on our starboard bow and two on our port beam. Instinctively looking upwards, I saw a single Heinkel bomber thousands of feet up directly above us.

This attack, coming as it did literally out of the blue, shook me, and I suspect everyone else, to the core. I have never seen such a lot of scared faces, and talk about "Jumping out of one's skin!" The fact that the attack had been carried out unobserved, and that we had not opened fire either, added to our mortification.

From mid-June onwards we received a stream of orders, under the heading operation "Purge". These orders were to come into force in the event of a sea-borne invasion. Briefly, the idea was that every available ship was to put to sea at once, continue firing till their ammunition was expended, and then sink the invasion craft by ramming them. There was a code-word in the orders which signified: "I have sighted a suspicious number of unidentified ships" and this was to be made immediately if such an occasion arose.

One dark moonless night steaming along off the Norfolk coast with a southbound convoy, the shape of a large number of ships became visible in the gloom ahead of us. The movements of our own forces were known to us, and we had not expected to sight any at that moment.

On the bridge of *Black Swan*, the Captain and I peered with eyes straining through our glasses to identify them. There was a tense silence, broken only by the rumble of our director slewing round to get the guns trained on this unknown target. In my mind's eye I could see the whole nation springing to the Alert on receipt of one signal from *Black Swan*. The code-word was, appropriately enough, "Blackbirds"!

"Main armament ready, Sir," came the report.

"Make the challenge, signalman," rapped the Captain.

Clickety-click-click went the small blue-shaded lamp.

"Challenge made, sir," said the signalman, quickly.

We held our breath, then an answering wink came from one of the dark shapes ahead of us.

"Reply correct, sir," sang out the signalman. Audible sighs of relief went round the bridge. The "enemy" turned out to be a northbound convoy several hours ahead of time-table.

In the first year of the war on this route, convoys invariably met at night on opposite courses generally near a buoy on a corner of the route. Eventually the southern half of the route was doubled up with a one-way traffic rule, so that these appalling nightly meetings were avoided in that area anyhow.

In October, 1940, our Captain, Captain Poland, left *Black Swan*, and Commander H. P. Henderson assumed command of the ship at Rosyth. We sailed next day on a southbound convoy which was uneventful, and returned northward as usual about six days later. It was on the morning of November 1st, that we were steaming up the Firth of Forth, glad that another convoy trip was behind us and looking forward to a day or so in harbour.

My cabin was aft, above the wardroom, on the upper deck level, and about eleven o'clock I was sitting there at my desk when some lucky instinct prompted me to go out on deck. I had just risen from my chair when there was a tremendous explosion, and the whole stern of the ship seemed to spring out of the water.

I was catapulted through my cabin door, and the chair and my desk followed me. For a few seconds I could not think what had happened. All the lights had gone out, but the door to the upper deck was open, and I could see along the passage. Through a haze of dust, I saw the leading cook peering with an astonished look on his face out of the galley.

"We've been mined!"

After the initial bang, there was complete silence, and I could feel instinctively by the lack of vibration that the engines had stopped. I thought to myself—"Now don't get in a panic," and stepped back into my cabin for a torch. Then I hurried to the top of the ladder leading down to the cabin flat and magazine. In the darkness below I could hear men shouting and a few groans. Down below I met Johnnie Duggan.

"What the hell's happened, sir?" he said.

"Are you all right?"

We spoke simultaneously.

"Yes, sir, but there's somebody here been hurt."

I could see several men lying round about in the cabin flat, and then the Engineer Officer appeared.

"Quick, Chief," I said, "see if there's any water coming in aft."

Two ratings ran down the ladder from the upper deck, and a steward came out of the pantry.

"Get these fellows who've been hurt up top," I said, "as quick as you can."

The Gunner, Chief and I went down aft in the darkness. It seemed terribly quiet and unpleasant. We hurried round, calling out to see if anyone had been trapped in the after store-rooms or magazine. To our relief, there seemed to be no major flooding anywhere. Several ratings had been wounded, but nobody was killed. The mine had gone off under the stern, and the force of the explosion was vertically upwards. Concussion and broken ankles were the main injury.

A shelf full of books had descended round the Gunner's ears as he was seated in his cabin, and he was crowned by a volume of K.R. and A.I., which appropriately added insult to injury. But as his cabin was on top of a magazine full of ammunition, which was unaffected, he was considered lucky to have got off as he did. Anyhow, as he remarked, it wasn't the first time the book had given him a headache.

I ran up on the bridge and reported to the Captain what had happened. To avoid further damage to the engines, he anchored the ship until tugs arrived and towed us safely into Rosyth. On arrival alongside, a cloud of depression settled over the ship. Relief at getting into harbour after the initial shock, combined with the anger at our ship having been damaged again, produced a feeling of despair and uncertainty. I think most people hit the bottle fairly hard that night.

Being mined is not particularly amusing. The unexpected-ness of the thing leaves a permanent psychological effect, how-ever slight. I know that even today any sudden thump auto-matically sends my mind back to that November morning in the Firth of Forth. There is the feeling that one's own stupidity has caused it, the annoying feeling that accompanies being out l.b.w. at cricket. There is the added annoyance of having had a kick in the pants from the enemy without being able to hit him back: a distinct loss of dignity about it. But—as always—a touch of humour rode side by side with this mis-fortune, for, a couple of days afterwards, I had a letter from an aunt of mine living in the depths of Buckinghamshire—a dear old thing, who wrote very sentimental letters.

"Dear Willie (I read),

"This is the first of November, and I am writing to wish you a happy month. I know your work at sea will be very arduous and wearisome, but I am sure the knowledge that what you are doing is in the right cause will be a great uplift to you. . . ." I'd had the uplift all right!

Black Swan was towed round to Dundee for repairs and, after a most hectic week of de-ammunitioning and de-storing, entered the Caledon Shipbuilding Yard. All officers and ship's company left the ship or went on leave, except for a skeleton maintenance party consisting of the Engineer Officer, Guns and myself and about twenty ratings. Life in Dundee was gay in those days, and as January passed I had an uneasy feeling that I was having too good a time. I wanted to be back at sea again, particularly as a half-stripe now adorned my sleeve.

Reading the reports of battles on the East coast against the Germans' latest menace, the E-boat, whilst I was living on the fat of the land—and it still was fat, too, in Dundee then—disturbed my conscience. I went down to the C.-in-C.'s office at Rosyth to see what I could do about another appointment; there I met Captain Ralph Kerr who was the Captain (D) Rosyth.

"With luck you ought to get a seagoing command," he said in a kindly voice, adding with a smile, "I'm hoping for one myself soon. I expect there'll be enough for both of us though."

His little joke had a tragic sequel, for he was appointed in command of H.M.S. *Hood*, and lost his life when she sank with all but three of her crew a few months later.

On January 28th, 1941, I was appointed in command of H.M.S. *Guillemot*, a corvette based on Harwich and employed on the East Coast convoy duties.

"Back on the Tramlines again, sir," said the Gunner, handing me the signal.

I was very sorry to leave *Black Swan*. I had watched her being built; I had had my first experience of enemy action in her; and I had shared many adventures aboard her with a very good crowd of officers and men. She was a damn fine little ship, and only a sailor knows what those words really mean.

Chapter IV

THE LITTLE BIRD

I FETCHED up at Sunderland on a singularly foul day, with a bitter East wind and cold, driving rain. The grey smoky area of docks and shipyards presented a depressing background as I trudged along to the Naval H.Q. After a chat with the local Naval Officer in Charge, I was driven down to Greenwell's yard in a naval car by a perky, blonde little Wren. We had some difficulty in finding the ship, and bumped and lurched our way round over innumerable locks and level crossings. At last we found the *Guillemot* lying quiet and still in a sheltered corner of the basin.

"I'll go back and get your gear now, sir," said the driver.

"Don't worry," I replied—it was pouring with rain and nearly dark—"it can wait till tomorrow. You don't want to do another trip on a night like this."

"Oh, but I must, sir."

"Nonsense, Constance," I said, employing a favourite expression of mine at the time.

She looked at me, blue eyes like saucers, in surprise.

"How did you know my name was Constance?"

"We have our methods," I said, and left her to work that one out, whilst I stepped on board to deal with sterner problems.

I had met the *Guillemot* before, at sea on East Coast convoys: she was normally one of a flotilla of corvettes based at Harwich, and was only temporarily in Sunderland for a refit. Even in that somewhat depressing condition, she looked a trim little job—not unlike, in fact, a little sea bird asleep on the surface of the water, away from the turmoil of the war. I immediately christened her in my mind "the little bird".

Although very new, she had a good reputation on the East Coast, having on one occasion shot down a couple of enemy aircraft. My predecessor, Darell-Brown, was waiting for me in the wardroom, which was most conveniently situated on the upper deck. I had known D-B in the barracks at Portsmouth in pre-war days, where he was well known for his genial manner and strong sense of humour.

"Welcome to sunny Sunderland," he remarked, "My God, what a day! Come on in and have a drink."

In war time, taking over a new ship whatever her size was quite a business: the most boring item was mustering all the confidential books and signal publications. Eventually we ploughed through that: then we had a walk round the ship, and met the various officers. My Engineer Officer, Commissioned Engineer Tom Garnett, R.N. was the real destroyer Chief: efficient to the highest degree, loyal, well-mannered and with a strong sense of humour. Being older than myself, I was often glad of his shrewd advice on various problems that cropped up from time to time.

The First Lieutenant or Number One, Lieutenant Milner R.N.R. was a live wire in every sense of the expression. He coped very well with all the day-to-day queries that faced an Executive Officer in war-time: a lively and jovial type, he sported a magnificent beard.

Sub-Lieutenant Simmons, the Sub, was also an R.N.R.: he was a cheerful young man and a good seaman, if at times a bit forgetful.

Lastly there was the Gunner, Mr. Sangwell, R.N. (Guns): right on top of his job in harbour, a good watch-keeper at sea, and good company in the mess. In fact, we were a very happy little wardroom.

The ship's company numbered about seventy: the Coxswain—tall, fierce-looking and a fine disciplinarian—knew everything about everybody. Petty Officer Telegraphist Flanagan and Yeoman of Signals Mills—ratings on whom all Commanding Officers had to rely on very considerably in a small ship—were both quiet, good humoured and efficient.

"As good a ship's company as you'll get anywhere;" remarked Darell-Brown, "one or two scallywags, of course, but they turn up in every ship. You'll be absolutely all right as soon as you get her to sea."

Next day, after he had handed over the ship and made the necessary signal, I saw him off by train.

"All yours now, old boy!"

He waved cheerily from the carriage window as the train steamed out: with an odd feeling in my tummy I walked slowly back to the ship.

The refit was delayed as all refits invariably are by a variety of minor snags: in addition the weather played no uncertain part. In February of that year, 1941, there was a monumental snowfall in the North of England: the streets were literally two or three feet deep for several days. Snow was not the only thing that fell from the skies at that time, either: there were several air raids on the Tyne area.

Following our experience at Rosyth the previous year, I fully expected one of them on the second of March, when my wife came over to see the *Guillemot* for the first and only time: the ship sat, newly painted and with an air of alertness about her, all ready to sail in two days time for Harwich.

"She looks an awfully neat little ship," was my wife's comment, and neat was exactly the word for the *Guillemot*: Leading Steward Evans had got the wardroom shining like the proverbial new pin for a small party on the forenoon of Sunday, 3rd March.

We sailed next morning, having survived an air raid on Sunderland overnight, and went round to the Tyne to go over the D.G. range in the river opposite Oslo quay. This involved steaming up and down in the middle of all the river traffic, and I thought we were going to be involved in a collision at least six times. However, we survived, and went down river and out to sea past the breakwater, where we anchored to await a southbound convoy due at midnight.

The feelings of anyone taking their first command to sea for the first time, even under peacetime conditions, can only be understood by those who have had the experience. In wartime the responsibilities were increased a hundredfold, and to the natural feelings of pride and excitement at getting a command was added a modicum of nervousness at the thought of losing it. For when you go to sea, from the moment the engines start turning to the time when you ring off on return to harbour, the responsibility is entirely yours. There is no respite for one second. It is like driving a car non-stop night and day, a nautical car worth a great deal of money, with a crew whose lives are infinitely more valuable.

The slightest error of judgment on your part and the whole lot can be lost. And even when you are off the bridge—since everyone is human and must sleep now and then—the ship is still yours. If the Officer of the Watch makes a mistake, it is your mistake; and, by golly, it was easy to make them on the East coast in war-time. A silent prayer for Divine guidance often passed through my mind at sea during the war, but never more vividly than when I went up on the bridge just before midnight on March 5th–6th, 1941.

The *Guillemot* weighed anchor then, and set off quietly through the darkness to rendezvous with the convoy. Soon vague shapes appeared out of the dark from the northward: dimmed red and green sidelights were burned for a few minutes as the ships from the Tyne joined up with the convoy, and then the whole collection moved silently and smoothly on through the night. A small light flickered from the leading escort.

"Glad to see you back," read the signalman standing beside me. "Take station astern and muster convoy at daylight."

Before sailing, all escorts were provided with a list of ships in convoy, and it was the duty of one of the escorts to muster them at daylight. The rear escort, or Tail-ass Charlie, generally did this.

The next day passed without incident and I felt pretty well at home after a few hours. At tea-time the Chief came up on the bridge.

"Things are pretty well squared off now in my department, sir," he reported. "Everyone seems to be settling down all right again."

"We've been through all the gun drills, sir," added Number One, a few minutes later. "One or two of the chaps were a bit dreamy after the fleshpots of Sunderland, but Guns has given them a good shake-up."

Guillemot's armament was not very extensive: a single 4-inch gun forward of the bridge with very unbusinesslike control, an Oerlikon amidships, and a quadruple 0.5-inch right aft. On the bridge were a couple of Bren guns each side; they were unofficial armament, and had been pinched from somewhere or other.

"Good show," I replied. "Well, we'll go to night action stations when we reach E-boat Alley and see what happens,"

A quiet night followed with no alarms and excursions, for which I was duly thankful. When dawn arrived it was cold and wet with low cloud, ideal conditions for attacking aircraft. About half-past eight the guns' crews closed up again, as was the usual drill. I left the bridge, and was having a quick walk round the upper deck to see how they were getting on, when a signalman ran up with message. "Owing to low visibility," I read, "all friendly aircraft have returned to base."

It was then that I had the most vivid premonition of what was going to happen. Maybe I am extra-sensitive, maybe it was just Divine guidance, but at that moment I knew in my mind that danger was threatening us. I nipped back on the bridge, and passed the word for all guns' crews to stand by for action.

"Aircraft in sight, port beam, sir!"

I whipped up my glasses, and immediately sighted a twin-engined bomber flying on a parallel course. It was only about two hundred feet up, and seemed almost stationary. The swastika was plainly visible on its starboard side. For a second I stared at it, absolutely spellbound. I simply could not believe my eyes. Then it turned and flew right at us: I could hear the growl of its engines.

I yelled "Open fire!", and at once every gun in the ship fore and aft opened up. Signalman Jones leapt to the port wing of the bridge, and let fly with the Bren guns. Through my glasses I could see a hail of bullets producing little popples of flame along the fuselage of the bomber. Then I suddenly realised it was going to fly right over the ship.

"Full ahead together, hard-a-starboard!"

Guillemot had a covered-in bridge. Therefore, for one horrible instant, the aircraft was out of our sight as it roared a few feet overhead. I dashed over to the starboard wing of the bridge, just in time to see four bombs exploding a cable clear on the beam. Then the aircraft collapsed in mid-air like a shot partridge, and followed the bombs into the sea. A man jumped clear a split second before it hit the water.

"We've shot it down, sir!"

The Sub was beside me yelling with excitement. I looked aft, and saw the First Lieutenant running along the upper deck, his mouth open in a soundless bawl, and pointing out to starboard where some wreckage was visible in the water. I felt like shouting myself.

"Engines going full ahead, sir, wheel still 'ard a starboard." The Coxswain's quiet voice brought me back to my senses.

"Stop both engines! Midships the wheel! Half-astern together! Away lifeboat's crew!"

In a flash the whaler was full of volunteers, and the news spread quickly round the ship. Men crowded up from their stations below, and I could see the Chief's head peering out of the engine-room hatch. I stopped the ship near the wreckage, and one man was seen swimming around. The whaler soon picked him up, returned to the ship and was re-hoisted. Then I got a bit of a shock—what with gyrating about and the excitement of the incident, we had lost touch with the convoy. The visibility was low and there was nothing in sight. We were in the vicinity of the Shipwash Shoals. My God, I thought, how awful if we run aground.

"Course to steer, sir, please?"

The Coxswain was looking at me interrogatively. I did some rapid mental calculation.

"Steer one-one-oh degrees."

"Very good, sir."

"That should bring us up to the Sunk Buoy, I think, Sub," I said as casually as possible. To my intense relief, the buoy soon showed up almost dead ahead. We increased speed, and in a short time caught up with the convoy. In the meantime we had sent out a brief signal to shore authorities, "Attacked near Sunk Buoy. No damage or casualties. Aircraft shot down, one survivor picked up." As this was made on a wavelength on which every destroyer in the vicinity would be listening to, our fame spread far and wide!

"Congratulations. What-did-you-hit-him-with?" flashed the destroyer *Eglinton* a few minutes later.

"Everything except the galley stove," was our reply.

The German we picked up was unhurt but in a miserable state.

"I've put him in the galley to dry off, sir," said Number One, coming up on the bridge.

"Go on, Sub," I said, "you fancy yourself as a German linguist, go and see what you can get out of him."

The Sub took his uniform jacket off, and donned an old sweater to hide his rank. Then he went down and engaged the enemy in casual conversation, but the results were not outstanding. The only intelligence gained from the enemy was an envious "You-feed-blotty-well", as he gazed at the ship's company dinner being prepared.

Shortly after this incident, we were ordered to leave the convoy and proceed to Harwich. The entrance into harbour was a bit tricky, but any fears I had of taking the wrong turn were soon allayed by the Coxswain.

"The last Captain used to leave it to me, sir," he said respectfully, "I knows it like the back of me 'and."

So, as the wheel was on the bridge beside me, I left it to the Coxswain, although I kept a very careful eye on things. By five o'clock we were secured to our buoy in mid-harbour, and I rang off the engines with an inward sigh of relief at a first trip successfully completed. Moreover, there was a very happy sequel. One of the local staff officers, Shawcross by name, arrived on board to get details of our shooting affair.

"I'll see if I can get it on the nine o'clock news tonight," he said.

"Be a sport and send a wire to my wife telling her to listen, will you?" I said.

He did so, and the wire arrived next morning! However, she was luckily listening-in by the fire at home that night, when she heard the following among the headlines, "An enemy bomber was shot down by one of our Naval Escorts in the North Sea this morning."

She told me she was absolutely certain it was the *Guillemot*, and sure enough in the amplifying announcement a few minutes later, the ship's name (and mine as Commanding Officer) came through on the air! My wife confessed that she took the wireless set upstairs to her bedroom merely to hear the bulletin again at midnight; I suspect that under the circumstances most wives would have done the same. A few days later I received a greetings telegram from the *Black Swan*: "Congratulations from one bird to another!"

The Heinkel incident was a very lucky start to my time in command, and everyone on board was in high spirits as a result. The story went round the flotilla in no time at all, and improved considerably with the telling. The others in the flotilla were *Puffin*, *Widgeon*, *Shearwater*, *Sheldrake*, *Kittiwake* and *Pintail*. We were a happy party under Commander E. H. Hopkinson in *Sheldrake* and I look back on my six months there as one of the happiest and most exciting periods of my career. Apart from duties with the convoys, we often accompanied mine-layers out when they were laying the North Sea mine barrier, which was tricky work.

Our first trip was one of those, and after it was over we returned to the Humber, and proceeded up river to Immingham in company with a Free French destroyer. The first night in harbour the Admiral in charge of the base kindly invited officers from both ships to his house for a cocktail party, where we met some very charming Wren officers.

"I hope you don't mind, sir," said the Chief later that evening during supper on board, "but, acting purely in my capacity as Mess Secretary, I asked some of the Wren officers to come down here after supper tonight. In fact," he added, "they're due almost any moment."

"Nice work, Chief," I said, "all for it."

Half a dozen smiling Wren officers duly arrived, followed shortly afterwards by an air raid warning. The enemy were dropping mines in the Humber, but luckily none came down by us, or if they did, we never heard them. Next morning a signal was received that the port was closed due to these mine-laying activities, and *Guillemot's* departure was postponed for twenty-four hours.

"Good show," said the Sub. "Fix another party for tonight, Chief."

"Well actually, sir," said the Chief, coughing gently, "acting——"

"—purely in my capacity as Mess Secretary," we all chorused loudly.

"—I did suggest," went on the Chief, ignoring the interruption, "that if our departure was postponed, we would be very glad to accept their kind invitation to visit their mess ashore tonight."

So up we went to the Wren Officers' Mess, and had a very pleasant evening. There was an illustration in the *Sphere* that week, by one of their staff artists, of his impression of the

Guillemot shooting down the Heinkel. Pamela Walker, one of
the Wren officers, cut it out, pasted it on a sheet of cardboard
and wrote across the top "Well done! Best of luck from the
W.R.N.S. officers, H.M.S. *Beaver II*. It was a nice little gesture,
and when we left after the party she kissed me good night,
which was even nicer.

"Take care of yourselves," she whispered, "and come back
soon."

Despite Pamela's good wishes our next trip was nearly our
last. We were with a northbound convoy off Lowestoft when
darkness fell on the two lines of ships doing their usual speed
of seven knots, but making little headway against a strong tidal
current. Most of the ships were in ballast, their propellors half
out of the water, and the overall impression gained was that
the whole lot were stationary. It was a pitch-black night, calm,
and not a breath of wind—ideal attacking conditions for the
E-boats.

About ten o'clock there was a heavy explosion ahead, and a
ship hauled out of the line and stopped. The RT receiver on the
bridge started crackling... "E-boats starboard side of convoy."
Tracer bullets were seen flying through the darkness, and dull
booms indicated starshell were being fired. A few seconds later
a bright yellow glare spread all round the horizon.

I looked round and sighted two E-boats making off to the
eastward. We altered course towards them, increased to full
speed and opened fire with star-shell. Our maximum speed
was only 16 knots, but by keeping them illuminated, we gave
the faster destroyers a chance to close the range and engage
them with H.E. shells. We drove the E-boats off to the eastward, and their high speed soon outranged us. We fired a few
shots up their tails to encourage them, and then turned to
rejoin the convoy.

The star-shell had all gone out, and the night was blacker
than ever. On the bridge with straining eyes, the Gunner,
signalman and I peered into the inky darkness. Suddenly, to my
horror I made out the outline of a collier nearby on the starboard bow and steering a closing course. My heart went cold.

"Stop both! Full astern together! Hard a starboard!
Sound three blasts!"

I leapt to the wing of the bridge where I could get a clearer view; I felt literally sick as I watched the huge shape drawing relentlessly nearer. "Oh God!" I muttered.

The seaman on the wheel was a good lad but rather slow in the uptake, and the butt of many good-humoured jests by his messmates. Normally, when told to do anything he could be relied to do it wrong first time. But this was his big moment. He put the wheel to starboard, rang down Full Astern on both telegraphs, and reaching above his head, pulled the siren wire three times.

In an agony of mind I watched the collier getting larger and larger till its silhouette seemed to be towering above us. At last when the disaster seemed inevitable, the *Guillemot* gathered stern way and drew clear of the menacing horror which lumbered past a few feet clear of our bows. The splashing of her propellor was clearly audible across the water. I gave the order to stop engines and had a quick look round.

"No need to shave tomorrow, sir," said Guns brightly.

I could not even reply. My mouth was dry and my legs were like jelly. I had nearly lost my little bird.

As time went on we got to know the ships in convoy very well indeed. Their names became as familiar as old friends, and we scanned the convoy lists with interest. One of the main duties of the escorts of a convoy was to keep the ships closed up well together. A straggler not only ran the risk of being attacked and sunk unknown to anyone, but generally involved one of the few escorts staying behind to keep an eye on her. The escorts had authority to order stragglers into the inter-mediate ports on the route, but this was not a popular measure with the masters.

In cases of engine trouble, bad coal or heavy weather, some stragglers were inevitable. This was particularly so on the northbound trip when the ships were in ballast. One day off Yarmouth we drew up alongside an elderly coaster miles astern of the convoy, making about three knots with propellor high out of the water, thrashing away in the most inefficient manner.

"Can you go any faster?" I shouted through the megaphone. No reply. "Can you increase speed a bit, please?" No reply. There did not seem to be anyone on the bridge. Eventually, after some more ineffectual shouting, the wing window of the collier's bridge suddenly opened, and an angry red face appeared.

"What do you think I am," it roared, "a —— Spitfire?"

Then the window slammed again.

The corvette attached to each convoy was invariably stationed astern, and thus had the job of dealing with stragglers or casualties. It was a position also in which the Captain had to use considerable initiative in dealing with unexpected situations often to the extent of disregarding orders. The worst problems invariably presented themselves at night and in bad weather. Visual signalling at night was out of the question, except at very short ranges with a shaded light: and although complete wireless silence was not enforced, it was highly undesirable to make long signals (which had to be coded up anyway) which might betray position of the convoy. So all problems had to be dealt with promptly, and explanations left till later. Attached to the convoys at that time were three or four incredibly ancient ships (I believe they used to run on the Great Lakes). The sight of one of their names on the convoy list always produced groans of dismay on our bridge.

"Another straggler tonight, sir," remarked the Sub, as we formed up with a northbound convoy at the Sunk buoy, "good old *Winona* again."

It was blowing a stiff north-easter, and with all ships in ballast and contrary tides, the convoy was being tossed and blown about like a lot of feathers. Sure enough, when darknesss fell with the convoy ploughing along into the short, stiff seas off the Suffolk coast, our old friend fell further and further astern. We were steaming at slow speed and still gaining on her. The rest of the ships, gradually drew ahead into the darkness and out of sight.

"It's no good," I said suddenly about midnight, "tell the damn thing to go back into Yarmouth. We'll go with her."

After nearly capsizing as she turned, the ship fairly scuttled southwards with the wind and sea astern. We escorted her safely into Yarmouth Roads about midnight, and made a brief signal to that effect. By that time it was blowing a strong gale from the north.

"Now what, sir?" asked Number One as he came up for the middle,

"We'll totter out again, plug into this until we meet the southbound, and then tag onto them."

I had hardly made this decision when a signal prefixed IMPORTANT was received from shore.

"Rejoin your convoy at full speed forthwith."

"I can just imagine the fellow who made that signal," snorted Number One, "sitting by a nice warm fire with a whisky and soda in his hand——"

"——probably never been to sea in his life——"

"——never bothered to look at the weather report——"

"——telling us to steam at full speed into a northerly gale——"

We worked ourselves up into a fine fury: it kept us warm anyhow. We ignored the signal, reported to the Senior Officer of the first southbound convoy we met, and heard no more about it.

But gales were by no means the only headache. Fog was even worse: for large numbers of ships to keep moving close together in the narrow confinement of the Tramlines in fog or low visibility was to invite disaster, either by collision or grounding. Many instances of both occurred: hence it became the rule for the senior officer of the convoy to signal the ships to anchor when fog came down. In 1941, before R/T communication was the vogue, the signal was passed by light or sounding of sirens. As often the convoy stretched for over five miles, by the time the signal reached the rear ships, a fine schemozzle had occurred. How there were not even more collisions than there actually were was always a mystery to me.

But even when the convoy was safely at anchor, there was no real relaxation. For lying at anchor, out in the open sea, with enemy torpedo-boat bases not so very far to the eastward, was not very comforting. The ships were literally sitting targets, and it always amazed me that the enemy did not send his E-boats over in daylight conditions of low visibility.

Had they done so, they would have found the ships in convoy completely at their mercy when at anchor. It would have been mass murder, with the escorts virtually powerless to intervene.

But, thank goodness, in daylight the E-boats never came.

CHAPTER V

THE MOON, MINES AND MUDBANKS

A T THE other end of the weather scale we got no respite, either.

"Full moon tonight, sir," remarked the Sub, as we joined up with our southbound convoy off the Humber.

"It'll be as clear as daylight," I said, "I wouldn't put it past the Hun to try an attack."

Sure enough, as we were on the southerly leg of the route beyond the East Dudgeon, two aircraft came in low from up moon. They circled the convoy in a leisurely fashion like a couple of Solway geese coming into the marsh. A tremendous shower of tracer went up, but they attacked through it, and then there were some heavy explosions ahead of us.

"One ship stopped, sir—Red one-oh degrees."

"She's hit, too."

We closed the casualty: in the bright moonlight I could see she was listing heavily, and a boat was pulling away from her side.

"Stand by to pick these chaps up."

I manœuvred the *Guillemot* as close as I could to the ship's boat, and stopped engines. Suddenly the Sub gave a shout.

"Aircraft port beam, sir!"

I leapt to the voice pipe.

"Full ahead together!"

The roar of engines, the rattle of our after guns opening fire, and the explosion of the bomb close astern were practically simultaneous. The little ship almost jumped clear of the water with the concussion and the full thrust of the propellors combined.

"Hard-a-starboard! Keep an eye on that boat somebody."

We did a complete circle; on completion of it we found that the merchant ship had disappeared: luckily the boat was visible, a tiny black eggshell sitting on the silvery water. I stopped the ship again and the men clambered aboard quickly. I saw them in a confused crowd on the deck amidships: there seemed to be an awful "confab" going on.

"What's up?" I called out from the bridge.

"Can't get no sense out of them, sir," replied one of our leading hands.

"Go down, Coxswain, and see what's up," I said. He turned the wheel over to a seaman, and jumped down the ladder: in a few minutes he reported back again.

"They're Norwegians, sir," he said. "One of them's in rather a dicky state—been burnt."

"Take them in the wardroom and do your best."

"Aye, aye, sir."

The Yeoman of Signals tapped my arm.

"*Verdun* on the starboard beam, sir."

I saw the familiar silhouette of one of the Rosyth destroyers gliding past: a violet lamp was winking from her bridge.

"There-is-another-boat-to-northeastward-of-you," read the Yeoman.

"O.K. Where are we now, Sub?"

"Half-way between 58 A buoy and the next one, sir."

"Know where that ship sank?"

"Roughly, sir."

"Make a note of it. We'll have a look for this other bloke. Pass the word to all the guns crews to keep their eyes skinned."

We steamed off scanning the horizon carefully; at last, after a good deal of hither-and-thither business——

"Here we are, sir," sang out the signalman. Just off the starboard bow was another cockleshell looking extremely lonely. We stopped, and half a dozen men scrambled on board.

"Tell them we've picked their pals up," I said.

But I was wrong: they were Englishmen from a different ship altogether, which had also been hit and sunk.

"Cripes," I said, "I wonder where the hell it went down."

We searched around for half an hour or so, then set course to rejoin the convoy.

The sea was comparatively shallow in that area, and sunken ships were frequently a menace to navigation: if a mast or superstructure was visible above the water, the position was clear and could be marked by a light buoy flashing an appropriate warning at night. These wreck-marking buoys were painted green, and their flashing light was also a green one. As time went on, the area of the convoy route in the region of the Humber—Sheringham—the Wash, became a positive Piccadilly Circus of flashing green lights. But those ships which sank without trace, whose positions were not accurately known, were the real dangers.

As we rejoined the convoy we made a signal to base giving the names of the ships sunk, and their approximate position. A few days later in the operations office at Harwich, one of the staff officers called me over.

"This signal of yours;" he said, "we want the accurate positions of these sinkings. You want to have a Dan buoy all ready and drop it as close as possible when a ship sinks. That's your job in the rear position of the convoy—it's perfectly simple."

"Excuse me," I interrupted, "have you been on any of these convoy trips yourself?"

He looked rather surprised.

"Well, no—I haven't actually."

"I recommend you to go one day, then—they're not always quite so simple as you think. Good morning."

I left the office quickly before my temper got the better of my manners: returning aboard, the Chief's beaming face soon dispelled all clouds.

"Good news, sir—boiler-clean after next trip. I've fixed it with the Flotilla Engineer, if you can confirm it with the Staffie."

"Not with the silly basket I've just been talking to," I said, "I'll dwell a short pause and see the head man."

However, the boiler-clean was provisionally fixed, and the news spread round the ship like lightning. Boiler-cleans came in rotation about every six weeks for the corvettes in our flotilla: the ship in question went alongside, was placed at extended notice for steam, and two-thirds of the ship's company went on five days leave. Number One and the Coxswain had the whole routine buttoned: before we even sailed every man on the leave list had his travel ticket and leave pass made out, and I have no doubt had managed to convey the good news to his family by his own particular secret code. For myself, I had noted that an Investiture fell due conveniently within the proposed dates, and by skilful signals, phone calls and so on, managed to get my name included, and my wife duly informed.

Our northbound convoy was uneventful, we duly transferred to the southbound off the Humber, and took up our usual station astern. As soon as the ship's bows were pointing southwards an ever-increasing atmosphere of boiler-clean expectancy pervaded the ship: it affected everyone, including myself, and we were caught napping. In broad daylight long before we expected the evening flight of bombers, an aircraft flew in low from the landward side on our starboard quarter. I flicked up my glasses, recognised it as a JU 88, and seized the microphone which communicated with the after guns.

"Enemy aircraft starboard quarter!" I sang out, "Open fire, open fire, open fire!"

I was jubilant in anticipation of success: it was a sitting shot for the 0.5-inch gun and the Oerlikon. To bag another bird would be a wonderful thing just before a boiler-clean.

Nothing happened: at that instant the two men manning the guns, doubtless daydreaming of home and beauty, were both looking the other way.

"OPEN FIRE! OPEN FIRE!" I bellowed.

Then I looked at the mike in my hand and swore violently. I hadn't switched it on! Too late I did so: by then the machine had whizzed low past our stern and was a mere dot in the distance. The astonished gunners got a few rounds off up its tail, but clearly did not connect. I was livid with the gun's crews, but even more so with myself.

It was a typical instance of life on the East Coast convoys then: a target presented itself for a few seconds only, and if you were not absolutely on the alert you lost your chance—or even your life. The hardest part of the convoy work was the eternal vigilance that had to be maintained for complete success.

I spent the whole of the night on the bridge, muttering "If only—if only——" to myself. Nothing happened, and by dawn I was worn out, but comforted with the thought of five days leave ahead. By midday, the boiler-clean signal, which normally came by W/T, had not arrived, and alarm and despondency spread round the ship. The Coxswain came up on the bridge, and peered gloomily over the side, as if hoping to see the signal floating on a wave top. However, about tea-time when we were approaching the Sunk Buoy off Harwich, which was our usual spot to break away from the convoy, the bell pealed joyfully from the wireless office.

"Boiler-clean signal, sir!"

The fellow might have been announcing a general armistice: in a flash the Coxswain was off the bridge, and a muffled cheer could be heard as the news spread round the messdecks. I read the signal with a great sense of relief: it was in the usual wording, repeated to C.-in-C. Nore: then I pointed the *Guillemot's* nose towards home, and increased speed for the last lap. As we approached harbour, a light flashed violently from the signal tower.

"Why-are-you-entering-harbour? Rejoin-convoy-at-once."

As I tried to hoist this in, the bell rang from the office: it's single funereal toll indicated bad news.

"Yes?"

"Signal from C-.in-C. Nore, sir, repeated F.O.I.C. Harwich. ' Remain with convoy till arrival at Southend.' "

"Oh my God! Send it up, anyhow."

As I studied the second signal, my heart gave a bound. Although we had received it after the other one, the time of origin was earlier: clearly therefore we should obey the later signal, which ordered us to boiler-clean.

"What are you going to do, sir?"

Number One's face was a picture of misery. I knew there would be fifty others like it on the mess decks.

"Carry on into harbour, of course. We've been ordered to boiler-clean—we bloody well will."

The signal station was still flashing angrily at us.

"Why-are-you-entering-harbour?"

The Yeoman had his hand on our lamps.

"What shall I reply, sir?"

"Reply—'In accordance with your signal'."

We steamed on into harbour: short of opening fire, the signal tower could not stop us, and once we were in harbour we would have a moral advantage. I knew how miserable the ship's company would be if the boiler-clean was cancelled, and I was not going to be bullied by anyone.

"The signal tower's still calling, sir," said the Yeoman again.

"Ignore them," I said defiantly, "we'll be out of sight in a minute."

Number One roared with glee.

"Nice work, sir!"

We zoomed up harbour, and went alongside the boiler-cleaning berth just as darkness fell. A junior staff officer was standing on the jetty.

"The Chief of Staff would like to see you at once, sir. He's very angry, sir," he added nervously.

"So am I," I said.

The entire ship's company seemed to be waiting on deck as I left the ship: the atmosphere was tense.

"Good luck, sir," whispered Number One.

Up at headquarters I was met by a fuming staff officer, but I soon had him cold. The evidence was all there in our signal log.

"Your signal was the later time of origin, so naturally I obeyed it. I imagined that after C.-in-C.'s first signal—repeated to you—that you had been through to him on the 'Ops' phone, told him you wanted us to boiler-clean, and then made your signal. The fact that we received it before the other one was nothing to do with us."

"All right," he said, "I see your point."

After I had left his office, I went into another one and picked up the nearest phone.

"Victoire!" I said when Number One answered. From where I was I could hear the ship's company cheering!

Leave did not actually start till next morning, and when I returned aboard I intended to turn in early, having had no sleep the night before: but as soon as I'd finished one drink, Number One and the others immediately handed me another with the single word "Victoire!" It developed into quite an evening.

The short spell of leave did us all a great deal of good, and with the coming of May, the situation somewhat eased; but navigation along the East Coast, with its swirling tides and many shallows and sandbanks, was a constant problem.

"What the hell are those chaps playing at?" I said crossly one morning on the bridge. I was dead tired after being up at all hours during a night of low visibility and rain, and now the first light of dawn showed four ships well to seaward of the convoy route, and bunched together in an alarming manner.

"If you ask me, sir, they're on the putty," said Guns, peering at the chart: we were coming down past the Shipwash sands at the time. He was quite right; they had wandered off the convoy route and piled up one behind the other. As it happened, the tide was falling, so they were stuck for several hours at least, if not for ever. I took the *Guillemot* over to stand by them, picking our way cautiously between the mudbanks.

"We'd better anchor," I said. "It's no good mucking about here under weigh; we'll be aground ourselves in two ticks."

We eased down, and the forward guns crew stood by the anchor. I leant out of the bridge window.

"Let go!" I shouted, then looked upwards. "No—as you were—full ahead together, hard a port!"

For at that moment a JU 88 slipped out of the clouds in a low dive. We gyrated round firing madly, while mudbanks whistled past us a few yards off. The aircraft dropped its bombs well clear, and after circling round out of range, low above the water, it flew off to the eastward. We steamed around for some time, and then anchored to seaward of the stranded ships, feeling remarkably naked with only a few miles of North Sea between us and the enemy. The Gunner and I looked at each other in silence.

"Are you thinking what I am?" I asked.

"Well, I dunno, sir," he replied laughing, "but if I was pilot of that aircraft, I'd fly home and say, 'Please, Mr. Hitler, there's four fat merchantmen stuck on the mud with only a tiny corvette sculling around—let's go and blast 'em all to hell!'"

"Exactly," I said.

We waited all day but nothing happened. As the tide rose in the afternoon, three of the ships floated off successfully and steamed away one after the other, like trams coming out of the depot. The fourth, however, stuck fast, and the falling tide rendered the position hopeless. She signalled she was shifting cargo, and hoped to get off at next high water.

"Oh dammit, that means another night on the briny for us," I said. "We can't very well desert this poor basket."

"The great ass," said Number One savagely, "what the hell were they all doing over here? It's two miles to eastward of the Tramlines. He must have been crackers last night. Just following the next ahead and never looking at the bloody chart. What shall we do tonight, sir? Stay at anchor, or steam around this fathead in ever-decreasing circles?"

My brain had been whirling round in ever-decreasing circles also, trying to decide what we should do. To stay at anchor was obviously the easier solution for us: the number of men on duty could be reduced, and we would have no navigational worry. We would also be in close contact with the ship aground. On the other hand, if some E-boats arrived, we would be torpedoed like a sitting duck. It was a perfect night for them, calm and low visibility. True enough we could keep a listening watch for them on our asdic set, but the operator had reported considerable interference from the swirling water, hissing and gurgling in the nearby shallows.

If we got under way and steamed up and down to seaward, we would be in a happier position as regards fighting off any E-boat attack—but at the same time with no nearby light to fix our position on, we might easily go aground ourselves, and in the low visibility we would soon lose sight of the ship we were supposed to be guarding: that is unless we made very short "legs" to and fro, which would be a frightful strain. An added menace was the East Coast mine barrier not far to the eastward of us: if we strayed into that we would be a dead duck in no time.

Would any E-boats be sent over? That was the crux of the matter: my head ached trying to weigh it all up: either way we would be wrong, and either way we were in for a miserable night.

"We'll stay at anchor," I decided, "with any luck we'll be left in peace. Have the usual gun's crews closed up, of course, maintain listening watch, and one officer is to be on the bridge all night."

"Aye, aye, sir," replied Number One briskly, "right, Sub, you take the first——"

"I ought to be taking that blonde Wren to the Club dance tonight," moaned the Sub.

"Some girls," observed Number One meaningly, "have all the luck."

"Think of all the money you're saving, too," added Guns.

"—and you, Guns, can have the middle," continued Number One, "I've just worked out the E-boats should arrive about one o'clock sharp, so don't go to sleep."

"Thanks a lot," murmured Guns, "and what about you, eh?"

"I *might* relieve you about daylight," was the reply; "depends what I'm feeling like. You can give me a shake about four just in case——"

"You bet I bloody well will," said Guns.

Darkness closed down, and the long hours of waiting began. It was chilly even for May, and a dampness hung over everything. Only the tick-tick of the gyro repeater broke the silence, as the signalman, look-out, Officer of the Watch and myself peered out into the night. Slowly, ever so slowly, the luminous hands of the bridge clock crept round. Somehow or other we hacked our way through the night.

"High water's about two a.m., sir," announced the Sub, "and if she doesn't get off then, it'll mean another twelve hours out here."

As two o'clock came along, we watched the merchant ship closely. Clouds of smoke belched from her funnel.

"She's moving, sir, I think," announced Guns.

"Thank God for that."

Suddenly to our horror, the ship started flashing at us with an unshaded lamp which had the dimensions of a searchlight.

"Am-free——" began the signalman.

"Tell her to switch off," I shouted, "they'll see that bloody light over in Holland."

We weighed anchor hurriedly and led the other ship back on to the convoy route: once back on the Tramlines, I heaved a sigh of relief.

"Tell her to follow us down to Southend," I added, "and, boy, will I be glad to see the last of her." Oddly enough, today I cannot remember her name: it was something like *Birkwood*. We reached the safety of the Thames estuary the next morning.

"Thank-you-for-standing-by-us," signalled the ship as she steamed up river, "best-of-luck."

Well, it was just part of our job, but it was nice to get such a signal.

"Reply—'Thank you. Same to you,'" I said yawningly, "'See you again soon'."

But we never did. The very next time she left harbour she was bombed and sunk. All our efforts had been in vain.

Toll was taken of escort and merchantman alike. One morning in harbour, Rupert Egan, Captain of *Shearwater*, came into my cabin and drew the curtain behind him.

"Bad news, Willie."

"What's up?"

"Mac's bought it. Mined last night off the Humber. Ship sank in two minutes."

"Mac" was one of our opposite numbers. MacClintock was his name, and he was Captain of *Pintail*, one of our corvettes. The trip before, *Pintail* had performed a remarkable feat of salvage towing a damaged tanker into the Humber.

"How many survivors?" I asked.

"Twenty."

"Was Mac saved?"

"No, the midshipman was the only officer picked up."

"Old Stanley's a goner then, too?"

"'Fraid so."

"Oh hell!"

We sat in silence for a few minutes. Stanley Paris was the Engineer officer, an old shipmate of mine in the *Marlborough*. He was one of that grand type of destroyer "Chiefs" that I have referred to previously. At once I had another thought.

"This is awful; his wife lives here, you know. Has she been told yet?"

"Don't think so: it hasn't been made public yet. One of the 'staffie's' told me. I thought I'd let you know. You and Stanley were old shipmates, weren't you?"

"Yes—in the *Marlborough* when I was a midshipman."

My mind flashed back over fourteen years to an evening in Wrexford's Cabaret in Malta. I had been buying far too many drinks for some girl in there, and had run out of money. Stanley had lent me two bob to get back to the ship. I smiled as the memory came back to me.

Rupert stood up, "Well, I'll have to push off, old boy. Just thought I'd let you know about it."

"Thanks very much, old man."

After Rupert left, I stood gazing out of my cabin porthole with a heavy heart. Stanley and his wife shared a little house outside Harwich with another Naval couple called Westbrook. Mr. Westbrook was Chief of the *Puffin*. He would be sure to hear the news of *Pintail's* loss somehow, and would be in a terrible position until Mrs. Paris had been told about it. Sometimes the Admiralty telegrams to next-of-kin took days to reach them, particularly when changes of address were involved, which I happened to know was the case in this instance.

Mrs. Paris was a grand cheerful woman in her forties, and very popular in the flotilla. There was nothing she liked better than to have young officers and their wives or Wren girl-friends from the Base, along to her house at any time. Only the week before I had been there for tea with a crowd of fellows after a football match. After Rupert had left my cabin I went up to the Base and discussed the matter privately with the Admiral's secretary, Andy Price, who was a friend of mine.

"I feel I ought to go and tell her," I said. "You know what this telegram business is, it may take a day or so, and in the meantime she'll probably hear only a vague 'buzz' which will be worse still. You know how these rumours get around in no time, particularly bad ones. I'm an old friend of the family, and I feel I ought to do it right away. We're off to sea tomorrow."

"I think you're right, old boy, but I don't envy you."

I borrowed a bicycle and set off. Halfway there I felt it was going to be far too much for me, and I nearly turned back, but somehow found myself at the gate. Mrs. Paris opened the door. To my relief I saw Mrs. Westbrook behind her in the hall.

"Oh, hullo, Captain," said Mrs. Paris gaily. "Come in and have a cup of tea. Mary and I are just making it."

"Just a moment—I must have a word with Mary——"

I could hardly speak. I took the other woman by the arm and led her into the kitchen. As soon as I had shut the door I gasped: "It's Stanley—lost yesterday——" and told her the rest as briefly as possible.

Mary's eyes filled with tears.

"Poor Stanley," she whispered. "Oh, how awful!"

I tried to pull myself together. "Give me a cigarette will you? I must get it over quickly."

We went into the drawing-room. Stanely's wife was standing by the fireplace. I went up and took her arm. For a few seconds I simply could not speak. Then I forced the words out somehow.

"I'm afraid I've got bad news for you——"

"Is it Stanley?" The words came in a tiny flat voice.

I nodded. I tried to say something, but again the words would not come out. I put my arm round her shoulders, and with Mary at the other side, we sat down together on the sofa. I thought she might faint, but she sat bolt upright though I could feel her quivering.

"Is there no hope at all?"

"'Fraid not. Only wish I could say yes."

She took my other hand in both of hers and gripped it tight. We sat in silence for a minute.

"What about the others?"

It was characteristic of her to think of them almost at once.

"Only twenty saved—midshipman and nineteen men—the ship was mined—she sank in half a minute—it was all over in a flash." I gabbled the words out somehow.

"Poor boys!" She put her head on my shoulder, and started to cry quietly. I held her close and tried to comfort her. Mary slipped out, and came back with some tea. I gulped it down, and then glanced at my watch.

"I must go now. Mary's here with you. She'll stay. We're all most terribly sorry——"

With a final squeeze of her arm, I stood up and left the room quickly. There was no more I could do.

It was a perfect summer evening as I pedalled slowly back along the country lanes. The birds were singing, and from the hedges on either side, the scent of the dog-roses filled the soft, warm air. I swore savagely and uselessly to myself as I rode along. "Oh God," I muttered, "why must these things be?"

All over the world, I suppose, millions were asking the same question.

Such sad memories were softened by the passage of time and the tension at which we all lived: not long afterwards I received a signal appointing me in command of the destroyer *Verdun* in the Rosyth Escort Force. Although this was a "step-up", I was very sorry to leave *Guillemot* with her grand little team of officers and men. I had only been in the ship six months, but I had learnt a great deal in that time, in more ways than one.

A month later I received by post a very fine silver cigarette-box, with the picture of a guillemot engraved on it: the ship's name and mine and the date 1941 were inscribed below.

"With best wishes," read the enclosed card, "from the ship's company."

A visitor to my home once remarked:

"By Jove, that's a nice box—solid silver."

"On the contrary," I replied, "it's solid gold."

CHAPTER VI

THE E-BOAT PROBLEM

FROM MAY, 1940, onwards E-boat attacks were the biggest menace that East Coast convoys had to face.

The E-boats—a name officially adopted in 1940 as an abbreviation for "Enemy War Motorboat"—were motor torpedo boats. Their German name was *Schnellboote*, and they were 105 feet in length, displacement 86 tons: they were built of wood of composite section U-form, and were exceptionally stout and seaworthy. They were armed with two torpedo tubes forward, one each side, and in addition they bristled with pom-poms and lighter automatic guns. Some of the E-boats were fitted up as minelayers, and both types were extremely fast: their maximum speed was about 38 knots.

With this high speed, fuel consumption was correspondingly high, and their range was limited. It was not, therefore, until May, 1940, when the Dutch bases of Ijmuiden and Rotterdam became available to the Germans, that E-boats began to worry the East Coast convoys.

Their first success was on the flotilla leader *Kelly*, which was torpedoed in the middle of the North Sea and heavily damaged. She did, however, manage to reach the Tyne after a perilous trip in tow, which lasted ninety-two hours.

The E-boats operated almost entirely under cover of darkness. During the summer of 1940, with its short nights therefore, there was no E-boat activity, and on our side of the Channel, we had time to build up an opposing force. Before the war it had been anticipated that German submarines would attack our coastal traffic, and a small fast motor anti-submarine boat had been developed, known as a Masby: but when it became clear that the enemy submarine had been driven away from our coasts, the Masby was converted into a Motor Gunboat (or M.G.B.) to tackle the E-boat. The first British base was established at Felixstowe in Essex: this was also the base for our own equivalent of the E-boat, the Motor Torpedo Boat, or M.T.B. Felixstowe Base was operational by March, 1940.

Until May, 1940, both our M.T.B.'s and our M.G.B.'s had had rather a dull time, as the enemy was out of range. But with the fall of the Low Countries new prospects were opened, and in addition both M.G.B.'s and M.T.B.'s played a prominent part in the evacuation of Dunkirk. From then on, these Coastal Forces played an ever-growing and prominent part in naval war history, both on the offensive and defensive. On the East Coast the battle against the E-boats started in real earnest in September, 1940, when the first night attacks on our convoys were delivered, four ships being sunk on September 4th. From then on, it was a ding-dong struggle until April, 1945.

At the start of it, the advantage lay entirely in the hands of the E-boats. They were small and extremely fast: their low silhouette made them almost invisible on pitch black nights. In 1940, the number of destroyers available for escort duty was lamentably low—two per convoy was the normal assignment, sometimes only one. To defend a convoy of thirty, forty or fifty ships under those conditions was ludicrous.

With their high speed, the E-boats were almost impossible to hit: for although a destroyer's main armament of 4-inch (or 4.7-inch) was on paper vastly superior, such an armament was not intended for high-speed targets at short range. The guns could not be trained round fast enough: quick-firing weapons like pom-poms, Oerlikons and four-barrelled automatics were needed against E-boats, and early in the war our destroyers were woefully short of them. At that time, also, many of the merchant ships were entirely unarmed and defenceless.

At this stage, too, there were no surface radar sets fitted in the escorts: some of the modern destroyers had Type 285 sets, but these were designed primarily for aerial targets, and were not very reliable for anything on the surface. The chain of radar stations on the East Coast was not yet in commission, so that no warning of E-boat attack could be passed to the escorts.

The convoy route was lit every five miles by flashing buoys, which were equally visible to friend or foe. In no time at all, the E-boats knew the Tramlines as well as we did, if not better. Their initial tactics were to steer westwards from their base until the convoy route was reached, and then lie in wait for the convoys by a convenient buoy. Indeed, at times, individual E-boats had the nerve to secure temporarily to a buoy, being thus rendered the more invisible by the shelter provided.

Aerial reconnaissance by day having already provided the E-boat with a good idea as to the time and direction from which the convoy would appear, the E-boat had then only to wait until the forms of the ships loomed up in the darkness: torpedoes were fired to "brown" the convoy, and then they were off home like lightning. Another plan of attack was to lay a few mines in the path of the advancing convoy, and a third alternative was to use both torpedoes and mines. In the early days, the first indication that the escorts usually had of the presence of E-boats was the roar of their departing engines, followed by heavy explosions from stricken ships in the convoy. In 1940 on the East Coast convoy route the E-boats sank seven ships, a total tonnage of 12,022.

The obvious opponents for the E-boats were our own M.G.B.'s: but in 1940 the officers and men of Coastal Forces were involved in a tremendous struggle in understanding and manœuvring their temperamental craft, and in working out the correct operational tactics. This involved hours and hours of nerve-racking tension and noise in bitter winter weather at sea, and station keeping at tremendous speed in close formation, when a single lapse of judgment could mean disaster. It speaks volumes for the crews of Coastal Forces that they achieved such remarkable efficiency in such a short time, and under such arduous conditions.

At first, the M.G.B.'s operated in company with destroyers on patrols to lie in wait and intercept the E-boats before they reached the convoy route: but this plan did not work, as the destroyers were not unnaturally averse to lying stopped in mid-ocean, thus presenting a perfect target, and when under way, the noise of the M.G.B. engines gave the position of the patrol away. So the M.G.B.'s operated by themselves in scattered patrols well out to seaward between the English and Dutch coasts.

The first of many M.G.B.-versus-E-boat actions came on 29th April, 1941. It lasted twenty-five minutes, and was inconclusive, but it was good practical experience. A second action, about a month later, lasted almost twice as long, and ended by the British M.G.B.'s pursing five E-boats practically to within sight of Ijmuiden.

During the summer of 1941, E-boat activity eased down as it had done the previous year. Meanwhile, we in the escorting destroyers were gradually acquiring more short-range weapons by every possible method, official and otherwise, and as more destroyers became available, the strength of the escorting force increased. Moreover, additional escorts were provided in the shape of trawlers and motor launches. These latter (M.L.'s for short) were akin to M.G.B.'s, but not so fast or well-armed. Every night at dusk two of these joined up from Lowestoft with the northbound convoy, and took station halfway down the column, or right astern, as close escort. Their main duties were to assist in A.A. defence, and to pick up casualties. After a night trip through E-boat Alley, they proceeded into Humber, and a day or so later repeated the performance with a southbound convoy back to Lowestoft.

In practice, the value of these M.L.'s was dubious, mainly from the point of view of their own safety. For in the event of an E-boat attack, they were very liable to be mistaken for E-boats and shot up: also, the noise of their engines was clearly audible in the earphones of the Asdic ratings on watch in the destroyers, and rather nullified their value, apart from causing false alarms. Still, their guns were very useful in joining in the barrage to greet dusk-attacking aircraft, and many hundreds of merchant seamen's lives were saved while these M.L.'s were with the convoys in 1941.

Meanwhile in August, 1941, a most distinguished young R.N.V.R. officer took over command of the 6th M.G.B. Flotilla at Felixstowe. He was Lieutenant Commander R. P. Hichens, and his courage and example dominated our Coastal Forces as no other officer ever did. He inspired not only his own flotilla, but those everywhere in the Service. For the next eighteen months, he was almost continually in action, being decorated five times in that period, before he was killed in April, 1943.

Such a leader was certainly needed on the East Coast when the winter of 1941–42 set in. It was one of the fiercest winters of the war, both from the point of view of the weather and enemy action. It was in the early hours of 20th November, 1941, when 6th M.G.B. Flotilla under Hichens scored their first decisive victory over the E-boats. After E-boats had attacked a southbound convoy and sunk two merchant ships: *Aruba* (1,159 tons) and *Waldings* (2,462 tons), Hichens took a couple of M.G.B.'s some twenty miles to the eastward of the convoy route, and stopped engines to wait for the E-boats' return.

When five E-boats appeared and lay stopped apparently at their pre-arranged rendezvous, the two British M.G.B.'s attacked at about fifty yards range. The enemy was taken completely by surprise, one E-boat was sunk outright, and another severely damaged.

Only nine days later, on 29th November, 1941, after a fierce attack by E-boats on a southbound convoy, two ships being sunk—*Asperity* (699) and *Cormash* (2,848)—a very similar action took place, with an interception off the Dutch coast. Though indecisive with damage and casualties on both sides, the knowledge that on every future sortie against East Coast convoys they were liable to be intercepted on the way home must have given the enemy considerable food for thought. Even so, in 1941, the E-boats sank twenty-three ships, total tonnage 48,888: five of these ships were sunk in one attack on March 7th.

Due to the bad weather E-boat activity was restricted for the next few months. It was not so much that Coastal craft on either side could not go out in bad weather as that it was impossible to manœuvre them at speed for fighting. On the East Coast, therefore, we in the escorting destroyers whilst heartily cursing the gales, were at the same time extremely thankful for them!

After a spell of nearly two months in which no operations were possible due to weather some E-boats attacked an East Coast convoy on 14th March, 1942. A single E-boat returning to its base was intercepted by three M.G.B.'s, and brought to a standstill by their gunfire. It was boarded, prisoners were taken, and an attempt made to tow the prize home: this was unsuccessful, however, as the E-boat sank and when four others appeared on the scene, our force suffered heavily in the ensuing engagement. However, all three M.G.B.'s returned safely to harbour.

On 18th April, 1942, some E-boats laid a minefield off the Suffolk coast, and the next day a southbound convoy ran into it. Two "Hunt" class destroyers were damaged, and two merchant ships sunk. *Verdun* was escorting this convoy, and it was on top of one of these two merchant ships that *Verdun* was nearly stuck for ever, as I shall recount later.

By this time however, our M.G.B. had developed a new stage in tactics: this was to try and intercept the E-boats before they attacked the convoys. On 21st April two pairs of M.G.B.'s lay in wait off Ostend, the most recently-formed base for the E-boats. A most successful interception took place against heavy odds, and after a fierce engagement the E-boats retired to base and did not come out again that night, or for many nights afterwards. It was a major victory for our M.G.B.'s.

By June, 1942, two new types of coastal craft had been built: the first was the Steam Gun Boat, more heavily armed and also carrying torpedo tubes: the second was an enlarged type of M.G.B., 71 ft. 6 ins. in length, with all the faults of the original boats remedied. Moreover the enemy was now well aware that our Coastal Forces were on the upgrade, and on the offensive on every single night that the weather would allow. In 1942, the E-boats sank eight merchant ships, total tonnage 13,725, and H.M.S. *Vortigern*, one of the destroyers.

E-boat activity against the East Coast convoys decreased until September. Then it flared up again, and continued all through the winter of 1942–43. Although every action was different, their overall pattern was more or less the same. The warning alarm by radar; starshell all round the horizon from the escorts, followed by heavy gunfire and criss-cross tracer in every direction; a dull boom as a merchant ship was torpedoed and sunk; then the retirement to the eastward by the enemy, and silence round the convoy still ambling along through the darkness: then, after an interval, an intercepted signal—"Am engaging E-boats in position——"; we in the escort would know that our M.G.B.'s had intercepted the enemy on his own

The author on leave near Stirling, August 1942.

H.M.S. *Bittern* ablaze in Namsos Fiord after having suffered a direct hit in the stern by a bomb.

H.M.S. *Black Swan* in the Clyde.

Broadside view of H.M.S. *Guillemot*.

Superstructure of wreck on the East Coast convoy route.

Last moments of H.M.S. *Salopian*, 13th May, 1941.

Greek vessel bombed night of 23rd October, 1941. Photograph taken from *Guillemot*, 24th October.

H.M.S. *Ulster* damaged by a 'near-miss' bomb abreast funnel.

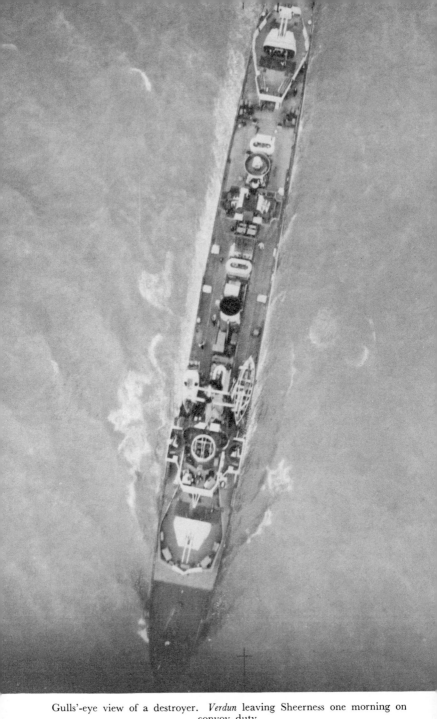

Gulls'-eye view of a destroyer. *Verdun* leaving Sheerness one morning on
convoy duty.

H.M.S. *Concord* oiling at sea from the cruiser H.M.S. *London*.

H.M.S. *Glengyle*, the author's last wartime ship, in the Suez Canal, 1941.

doorstep, and that an even fiercer battle was in progress out of sight over the eastern horizon.

It was not only on dark nights that the E-boats came over: if the sea was calm they sometimes came in the moonlit periods. One brilliantly clear night in the region of Smith's Knoll, we in *Verdun* sighted a couple of E-boats up moon of us: they were stopped and beam-on, a sitting shot. By that time most destroyers had been fitted with pom-pom or Oerliken guns right forward, or on the wings of the bridge as an anti-E-boat device.

This was just the occasion when they were needed. I increased to full speed, and we steered straight for the E-boats, everyone on the bridge shouting at the gunners to open fire. It was a freezingly-cold night, and the poor devils at the guns were so stiff with cold that they simply could not work the mechanism quick enough. As their gloved fingers fumbled with the triggers, the E-boats roared away to the eastward behind a smoke screen, and the chance of a perfect "right and left" to add to my sporting memoirs was gone for ever.

It was a typical E-boat incident, and typical also of life on the East Coast at that time. Long periods of being closed up at Action Stations at night in mid-winter were very arduous, and also boring when nothing happened. Sudden chances of scoring a hit against the enemy were few and far between, and when such opportunities came it was a question of being absolutely on the top line. A delay of a few seconds spelt the difference between success and failure.

But by the spring of 1943 the battle against the E-boats was slowly turning in our favour. We had more escorts per convoy, more guns and better radar sets: there were three flotillas of our coastal forces now, based at Yarmouth, Lowestoft and Felixstowe. Lieutenant-Commander Hichens had a worthy successor in Lieutenant P. G. C. Dickens, R.N., who led the flotilla from Felixstowe.

On 28th March, 1943, an attempted E-boat attack on a southbound convoy near Smith's Knoll was intercepted by a force of our M.G.B.'s; after a fierce action, one E-boat was sunk and the remainder driven off to the eastward. No ships in convoy were attacked that night.

E-boat activity on the East Coast dwindled to negligible proportions during the summer of 1943, but on 24th October— a calm moonless night—they came over in strength to attack a northbound convoy near Smith's Knoll. However, extra destroyers and units of our Coastal Forces were on patrol in anticipation. A night of almost continuous action ensued, no less than sixteen separate encounters being reported. Four E-boats were sunk for the loss of one British trawler. The convoy again had escaped without being attacked, and it was clear that the defence of East Coast convoys was drawing ahead of the attack. In 1943 the E-boats only sank one ship, of 4,581 tons.

Some sporadic activity occurred in the spring of 1944 and one ship was sunk of tonnage 2,085 but gradually the scene of action shifted down towards the Dover area, and with the invasion of France, every available E-boat was directed to attack the Allied shipping in the cross-Channel and Normandy beach area. During the winter of 1944–45, the East Coast convoys were virtually unmolested, except for a sudden flare-up in the early months of 1945, when five ships were sunk of tonnage 10,221. Several fierce battles were fought, but by April, 1945, the spirit of the E-boats was broken and all attacks ceased.

In addition to the many ships torpedoed by E-boats in their night attacks on the East Coast convoys, many were sunk also by the mines that they laid. The latter were of three different varieties: the Contact mine which floated a few feet below the water, held in position by a wire attached to a sinker on the sea bottom: the Magnetic mine, which lay on the sea bottom and was exploded by the magnetism of a ship passing over it: and the Acoustic mine which was similar to the magnetic sort, but whose firing mechanism was actuated by the vibration of a ship's propellers passing nearby.

Although many ships were sunk by mines, the work done by our minesweepers on the East Coast was magnificent. Day in, day out under the most arduous and dangerous conditions, the Tramlines were swept by minesweeping flotillas based all along the coast. Hundreds of mines were swept up or safely exploded before the convoys came along. Minesweeping was an essential if unspectacular part in the overall plan on the East Coast.

On the more active side, we in the destroyers and escorting craft did our best and helped in the actual defence of the convoys against aircraft and E-boat attacks. But there is absolutely no doubt that the final defeat of the E-boats on the East Coast was due to the work of the Coastal Forces flotillas from Yarmouth, Lowestoft and Felixstowe. Their skill and courage was beyond all praise: it was the same everywhere they went.

In the whole of the war our total Coastal Force strength developed from 28 craft and about 300 men to 1,500 craft and some 24,000 men. In over 460 actions in Home Waters, 269 enemy ships were sunk: this number included 142 E-boats for the loss of 76 of our own craft.

CHAPTER VII

THE ANCIENT WARRIOR

IN JULY, 1941, I joined H.M.S. *Verdun*. She was one of the oldest ships afloat, being an original member of the "V and W" class of destroyers, built in 1917. Between the wars, she had had the distinction of bringing home from France the body of the Unknown Warrior to his last resting place in Westminster Abbey.

For World War II, she had been converted to an A.A. ship with the latest fire-control methods. Her armament was two twin-four-inch mountings, one forward and one aft, and a few close-range weapons dotted round the ship. She carried depth-charges, but no torpedo tubes. Although twenty-four years old, she could leap around the seas at over 30 knots when required. Her class of destroyer was a triumph of British engineering skill: with proper care and maintenance they seldom, if ever, broke down and just went on and on like a trusty old car.

The Rosyth Escort Force was employed on East Coast convoy duties, mainly southwards from Firth of Forth to Thames. As I had been practically the whole war to date on the East Coast in *Black Swan* and *Guillemot*, I had no qualms about taking over the command of *Verdun*.

Rosyth was a good base, vastly improved from when I had last been there, almost entirely free from air raids and with plenty of amusements, both for officers and men. Edinburgh was close at hand for a real run ashore when the opportunity arose. Destroyers always berthed alongside, and on arrival in harbour were topped up with oil from a small local oiler, thus avoiding a trip to the large oiler berthed in midstream.

The Rosyth Escort Force was a very worthy flotilla in which to serve, and I was lucky enough to inherit as good a wardroom in *Verdun* as any C.O. could wish for. The Engineer officer,

"Chiefee" Seabrook, was with me during all my time in *Verdun*. He was a first-class man in every way, much the same type as Garnett in the *Guillemot*. A good messmate who kept a fatherly eye on the younger officers, he himself was not averse to joining in any ragging that went on: his smart russet beard was the envy of many another officer who tried to grow one.

Lieutenant Michael Marwood, D.S.C. was the First Lieutenant: tall and slim, he was a good seaman, and carried out his duties as Number One very well. He had a remarkable penchant for laying on wild parties, both on board and ashore, and an even more remarkable ability for emerging scatheless from all of them.

Another Lieutenant R.N. was Toby Rodwell, who was the Pilot and Signals officer. He had every detail of his job completely buttoned up from chartwork to knowledge of all the intricate signal procedure in force. At times his old-Etonian manner rather scared me, but he was a most likeable shipmate, loyal and amusing, and a good games player. An "old China bird" like myself, he and I used to spend hours on the bridge yarning about pre-war days in the Far East. We were so absorbed in this on one occasion, that between us we nearly involved the *Verdun* in a collision with a stray ship that suddenly loomed up ahead of us from nowhere.

Surgeon Lieutenant Philip Strang, R.N.V.R. was the Medical officer or Doc: small, with rather a shy manner at first, he soon blossomed forth into a very popular member of the mess, with a permanent twinkle in his eyes behind his spectacles. He took a great interest in every department outside his own, and was very popular with the ship's company.

There was a shift round of some of the junior officers soon after I arrived, but the newcomers turned out as satisfactory officers as they were messmates.

The ship's company, mostly from Chatham depot, numbered about a hundred and fifty; the Coxswain, Chief Petty Officer Guy, Chief Stoker Ranger, the Yeoman of Signals and Chief Boatswain's Mate were outstanding among the senior ratings. Among the junior seamen were about ten Australian and New Zealand men: they were all candidates for Commissioned Rank, and I had to interview them almost immediately I joined the ship. It was not an easy job, as I had only known them a few weeks, but I recommended each one of them for a Commission. In after years as the war went on, they all justified my recommendation to the highest degree. From time to time I had news of them; some of those who survived still write to me today. We finished our refit late in August, 1941, and we set off on our first convoy in good spirits. I had told the officers and ship's company about the success of my first trip in *Guillemot*, and said I hoped for the same in *Verdun*.

The southbound convoy was uneventful. On the second day of the northbound one we were off Berwick-on-Tweed at sunset. This was the ideal time for low-flying air attacks on the convoys, and we closed up at action stations in preparation for the evening flight. Sure enough, the sound of aircraft engines was heard through the gloom to seaward, and all guns were trained in the approximate direction. The noise grew louder and louder, then suddenly there was a tremendous splash and—silence.

"I believe he's flown into the sea," said the Pilot.

We steered towards the splash, and increased speed. In a few minutes, to our amazement, we sighted a Heinkel seaplane, nose down in the sea and sinking fast. Four men were clambering into a small dinghy.

At that time I was making a determined effort to learn German, so I seized the microphone and bellowed loudly *"Hande Hoch! Zie sind unser gerfengener."* If the Germans could comprehend my accent the sentence invited them to "put their hands up as they were our prisoners"—a pretty fatuous statement to make under the circumstances, but I hoped it might impress the *Verdun's* ship's company, if not the Germans. I never let on that it was practically the only sentence in German that I knew!

Anyhow, the four airmen in the dinghy paddled alongside, looking very sheepish and disgruntled when they came aboard. We learnt that while coming in low to deliver an attack, the pilot had misjudged the height and flown into the sea. Not a shot had been fired, but we claimed it as *Verdun's* bird. It so happened that we escorted into harbour a ship carrying a large supply of meat, and I could not resist making a signal to the local Naval-Officer-in-Charge: "We have brought home the bacon—and the swine."

An occasional change from the southbound convoys was the escorting of large ships northward to Scapa, or on trials, after emerging from the builders' yards on Tyne and Tees. One morning we were ordered to be off the Tyne breakwater at dawn to escort H.M.S. *Roberts*, a brand new "Monitor", while on her trials. It was a rather misty morning, and the sudden appearance of this huge ship out of the river entrance with her tremendous beam and bulges on either side, reminded me of a hippopotamus I once saw emerging from a swamp in Tanganyika.

We set off northwards on trials, and the Captain of the *Roberts* must have been feeling in good humour, for his first signal was: "As a blushing maiden we feel honoured at being escorted by such a hardy veteran."

This jovial comparison of the two ships called for a similar reply in my opinion, and we flickered back: "With a figure so flush, any maiden should blush." After that everything went swimmingly.

However, we kept our wit to ourselves on the next trip which was to escort the mighty battleship *King George V* up to Scapa. The return trip was made at night, in low visibility, and we passed into the Forth without being challenged by May Island. Halfway up to Rosyth, it came down much thicker, and we crept along at low speed, groping anxiously for the entrance through the anti-submarine boom.

This latter followed the usual pattern of such items, and was a massive affair of wire nets stretched across the channel under water, and supported by a line of buoys on the surface. In fog and low visibility, a look-out was always placed in the ship right forward in the bows to report any dangers lying ahead. On this occasion it happened to be a very natty young ordinary seaman with a public school and university education. A slight error in navigation brought us up to the boom itself, a cable or so clear of the entrance. Under the circumstances a professional seaman would have rapped out a loud report to the bridge——

"Boom right ahead, sir!"

Instead, from the darkness forward there floated aft in well-modulated and casual tones the somewhat remarkable statement——

"There's a sort of string thing in front of us, sir!"

We went astern in time to clear "the sort of string thing" and anchored for the night. When the weather cleared at daylight we discovered we were in the middle of a minefield. Not one of our best nights really.

Not long afterwards we got an even greater fright in Rosyth harbour itself. We had arrived in from a northbound convoy, and berthed alongside *Valorous*, who was already berthed alongside the jetty. It was a glorious, still day in October without a breath of wind.

During the forenoon Marwood came into my cabin and said he had arranged a hockey match against *Valorous* that day. Both ships were keen on hockey, and it promised to be a hard fought match.

"Hey!" I said, looking at the list of names in our team, "All the officers are down here. Who's officer of the day?"

Marwood shuffled his feet and coughed, "Well, sir, Lieutenant Rodwell is, but I was going to ask you if the midshipman could act as officer of the day for an hour while Rodwell's playing hockey."

We had an R.N.R. midshipman on board called Grist, who had just joined us. "We can't very well leave the midshipman by himself," I said. "It should be a commissioned officer, you know."

"Yes, sir, I know, but it's only for an hour. Besides we'll only be up on the hill in easy reach of the ship. *Valorous* think they're pretty good, sir. We want to see them off. Rodwell's one of our best players, as you know, sir."

I wavered. "Oh, all right. But he's got to come straight back on board after the match. No hopping into the Club for a drink, mind."

"Oh rather not. Thanks very much, sir."

It was a wrong decision on my part—a very wrong one, and I knew it. Once again I had a premonition that something frightful would happen. However, I ignored it and at that moment the harbour oiler secured alongside our starboard side with a bump, and put an end to our conversation.

It was a glorious October afternoon, mild and sunny without a breath of wind. We were playing away vigorously, when I suddenly noticed a huge column of black smoke rising up from the direction of the dockyard. As we were over the brow of the hill, we could not see where this column had its origin, and anyhow it was none of our business—or so we thought.

About ten minutes later a policeman came pedalling furiously across the playing fields, and dismounted on the touch line, panting and mopping his brow.

"Is-the-Captain-of-*Verdun*-here?" he gasped.

"Yes, what's up?"

"Your ship's on fire, sir!"

In all my naval career I do not think I ever felt so shattered. Five of us piled into Toby's car, and roared off down the hill towards the dockyard. As the latter came into view, flames and smoke could be seen erupting from the area of the destroyer pens. We all groaned in horror, and Toby pressed his foot flat down on the accelerator.

Suddenly—"It's not our ship," I shouted, "it's by another berth." Then I added, "It's not a ship at all; the sea's on fire!"

We fought our way through the crowd and ran on board. Toby dived down to his cabin to get on his uniform, while I ran along the upper deck to find out what had happened. The first person I met was the Commander-in-Chief.

"Where is the Captain of the Ship?" he was saying. "Where is the Officer of the Day? Is there nobody on board?"

A few questions, and I discovered the cause of the fire. When the oiler had finished supplying us in the forenoon, she had pushed off leaving a certain amount of oil floating on the surface of the water. By a thousand-to-one chance a tanker that had been carrying petrol had been washing her tanks through not far away, and there was a certain amount of petrol floating about as well, though that was not observed until later on.

In the afternoon, some of *Verdun's* sailors had been painting the ship's side, and one of them had thrown a lighted cigarette end into the water. It was quite a natural thing to do, and when the sea caught fire, his astonishment must have been quite considerable. This floating mass of oil and petrol flared up, and the schemozzle started. The wet paint along *Verdun's* starboard side began to smoulder, and the ensuing panic can be imagined. Fire brigades were summoned, all destroyers in the vicinity went to emergency stations, and bedlam broke loose.

Chief Stoker Ranger in *Verdun* was having a nap in his mess which was on the starboard side forward, above the magazine. He woke up and apparently reckoned it felt quite warm for October. Peering out of the port-hole, he looked into a solid sheet of flame. Whereupon, with great presence of mind, he ran aft, secured the keys of the forward magazine and on his own initiative opened the flood valves and flooded the magazine; thereby, of course, putting out of action for ever several hundred rounds of ammunition.

Meanwhile, the fire brigade had arrived, and with the help of others, played their hoses on to the flaming waters. The result was that a blazing, floating mass was blown away from *Verdun's* side, and drifted about fifty yards on to a Home Fleet destroyer which had just at that moment arrived from Scapa, and was about to secure alongside another pier.

Not liking her welcome, she pushed astern out of it quickly. The still-burning mass of oil then drifted on and enveloped the *Leeds*, an ex-American "Town" class destroyer parked in a little floating dock. To everyone's horror some depth-charges on her quarter-deck caught fire, and burned fiercely like Roman flares. When this happened, there was a general rush by those in the immediate vicinity to the nearest air raid shelter.

Down below in his cabin, Mr. Mason, Gunner of *Leeds*, was also having a snooze. He awoke and he too was surprised it had turned out such a nice warm afternoon. Then, running up on deck, he seized a hose and, switching on the water, made his way round the upper deck till he had put all the depth-charges out. For this action he was subsequently awarded an O.B.E. and he well deserved it.

Meanwhile the main fiery mass had drifted clear downstream and finally burnt itself out; but it was a real miracle that a disaster of the first magnitude had not occurred. If Chief Stoker Ranger had not flooded our forward magazine, *Verdun* might have blown up. In which case *Valorous* would have almost certainly blown up, followed by the *Leeds* and two other destroyers nearby. In fact it is no exaggeration to say that the whole dockyard might have been wiped out—a replica of the 1917 disaster in Halifax, when an ammunition ship caught fire and blew up after a collision in mid-river.

All these thoughts chased themselves through my head as I

sat in my cabin that evening, frantically typing a report of the proceedings to try and save myself from being blown up! I could not, of course, conceal the fact that I had only had a midshipman as Officer of the Day, and I groaned in agony at the thought of what senior officers would say when they heard about it. Next day a Court of Inquiry was held on board H.M.S. *Rodney*, under the Presidency of Captain Tom Troubridge to investigate the fire. Late in the afternoon I was called in, and after the normal questions——

"And who was Officer of the Day in H.M.S. *Verdun*?" asked Captain Troubridge.

"Midshipman Grist, sir," I replied.

"MIDSHIPMAN Grist?" said Captain Troubridge in amazement—and I can see his bushy eyebrows go up now as he said it, "a MIDSHIPMAN Officer of the Day in a destroyer?"

It was no good my trying to deny anything.

"Yes, sir—temporarily. I had given permission for him to take that duty for an hour while there was a hockey match on."

Only the scratching of the shorthand typist's pencil broke the ghastly silence that followed.

"Oh, I see," said Captain Troubridge, pursing his lips, "well, that will be all, Donald, I think."

There was really no need for me to open the door when I left the cabin!

After pumping out our magazine and renewing the ammunition, *Verdun* sailed next day on a convoy. All the time we were at sea, I was wondering what Captain (D) would have to say about it. On return to harbour I reported to him. After discussing the convoy, I said: "I'm very sorry, sir, that when the fire occurred last week, we only had a midshipman as Duty Officer. I had given permission for him to take the duty for an hour while one of the officers was playing hockey."

Then I braced myself for the blow to fall, but Captain (D) only roared with laughter.

"That's what always happens when you take a risk like that," was his reply. "Don't do it again."

Outside his door I mopped my brow with relief: but sometimes even now, I wake up in the night and curl my toes in horror at the thought of what might have happened.

Chapter VIII

WINTER ON THE TRAMLINES

THE WINTER of 1941–42 was one of the worst I can remember—in fact, as the war went on each winter seemed worse than the one before. Be that as it may, the long hours of darkness which the Captain of an East Coast convoy escort was obliged to spend on the bridge were a tremendous strain. Zig-zagging in confined waters either ahead of the convoy, or on its beam, meant terrific concentration; three minutes on one course, wheel over, then three minutes on the other leg, wheel over, and three more minutes, all through the night.

Half a minute too long on either "leg" and one might be involved in a collision, or end up in a minefield or a sandbank. The more experienced officers were being relieved by younger R.N.V.R. officers, the majority of whom were keen as mustard, but they could not be left on the bridge alone at night until they had had several months' experience of watch-keeping.

The night of November 19th, 1941, will live long in my memory. We had a large southbound convoy of over fifty ships, and we passed Flamborough just after sunset. It was a moonless period, with flat calm sea and not a breath of wind. Just before dark, the usual German reconnaissance machine appeared low down on the eastward horizon out to seaward, and flew up and down out of gun range. Darkness closed down on the convoy with an ominous inky black calm.

"E-boat attack for certain tonight," I remarked to the Sub.

Extra escorts had been sent from Harwich and Humber and took station at intervals all round the convoy, and so this great collection of ships groped its way through the silent night. The suspense of waiting for the inevitable attack was unbearable, and it was almost a relief when about nine o'clock off Sheringham the party started.

On that night *Verdun* was stationed astern the convoy. The main duty of the escort there was to prevent any E-boats sneaking in from the rear: a secondary duty was to deal with casualties. From the time *Wolsey*, the leader of the escorts, signalled the cryptic message: "E-boats in vicinity," and opened fire with star-shell, there was never a dull moment for twelve hours.

At least two separate groups of E-boats, four or five to a group, started to attack simultaneously, and a general melee began as escorts moved out to drive them off. The dull glow of star-shell lit up the horizon ahead; red, green and yellow tracers criss-crossed in all directions, and the heavy boom of gun-fire kept up an unceasing chorus.

All the time the convoy plodded slowly on through the night. The first casualty was an unexpected one, as in the heat of battle one of our destroyers, the *Campbell*, opened fire on the *Garth*, a "Hunt" class destroyer, whose smaller size and silhouette closely resembled an E-boat in the dark. *Garth* was disabled, and had to be taken in tow by a trawler—no easy feat in the dark with E-boats in the vicinity. A few minutes after this happened there was an almighty flash and an explosion ahead.

"That'll be that small tanker," said Toby.

At the same time a signal arrived from *Wolsey* telling us to keep a good look-out for an attack from astern. I rang up the after-gun mounting where the First Lieutenant had his action station. "Number One?"

"Yes, sir?"

"Don't look round now, but I think we're being followed," I told him. "Open fire without waiting for orders if you see anything coming up astern."

"Aye, aye, sir."

I replaced the phone, and found Toby nudging me. "Someone in trouble here, sir."

Through the darkness we saw a ship close on our bow. She was stopped and low in the water with a heavy list. The flickering of a torch showed on the waterline, and a boat pulled away just as the ship heeled right over and slid out of sight. Only a short hiss of escaping steam, like the sigh of a dying man, broke the silence.

We stopped close to the boat and I called to them to come alongside quickly. It was an anxious few minutes, for while we had no intention of leaving them to their fate, *Verdun* presented a sitting target to any lurking E-boat while we were stopped in the water. The boat was pulled alongside, and some men scrambled on board. I glanced at my watch as we went ahead again—only midnight—another seven hours to get through somehow. Ahead of the convoy and further out to seaward the battle was raging spasmodically. Much as we wanted to join in, our job was to stay in the rear of the convoy, zig-zagging to and fro to cover the last few ships.

"Hullo, here's another one," said Toby, peering through his glasses. "My God, there's an E-boat beside it," he added excitedly.

His remark galvanised everyone into action, but the E-boat turned out to be one of our M.L.'s, who called us up with a shaded blue light, and then came alongside. A few minutes later an officer appeared on the bridge.

"Could you send a Doctor and some ratings over to this ship, sir?" he asked quickly. "She's not too badly damaged, but they've got several chaps with burns. The master reckons with a bit of help he can get under way again soon."

We had an emergency party ready for such contingencies, and in a short space of time they leapt into the M.L. and disappeared over towards the dark form of the damaged collier.

"Wonder when we'll see them again," murmured Toby.

Short signals reporting the progress of the battle began to come in one after the other—"half-time scores"—as they were always referred to. Several ships had been damaged or sunk, but it was obvious the E-boats had not had it all their own way. The situation became more and more confused, and there were still several hours of darkness to get through. We pressed on through the inky night.

"Ship on the port bow and another on the starboard, sir," said the signalman suddenly. "Both steering to starboard, sir," he called.

I had just altered course slightly to pass half-way between them when a frantic flickering of Morse came from the left-hand one: "Keep clear, am being towed," read the signal. Just in time I put the engines to Full Astern Together, and we drew up a few feet short of the towing wire joining the two ships.

"Quite a party, one way and another," I said to Toby.

At that moment the bell on the telephone from the after gun rang furiously. The signalman answered it, then turned anxiously to me. "After gun reports E-boat coming up astern, sir!"

"Oh, Gawd!"

I put the wheel hard over and increased speed. The guns trained round and all eyes peered into the gloom. Astern of the convoy a small shape was seen frantically pursuing us—its silhouette seemed familiar.

"It's that M.L. we met just now, sir," said Toby.

He was quite right. The ship that the emergency party had boarded had been more seriously damaged than had been realised, and in spite of their efforts it had quietly sunk. We re-embarked our party, and pressed on at speed to rejoin the convoy which had now got some miles ahead of us. By this time most of us were getting a little worn. I looked at my watch—half-past three only—the night seemed endless.

"Small object bearing red two zero, sir."

Once again we were galvanised into action. I peered with straining eyes through my binoculars; the object certainly looked suspicious, and was moving quite fast away from us towards the convoy.

"Main armaments on, sir," sang out the gunnery control officer.

I was still not quite sure. We had gone on to full speed now, and were catching the object up from astern.

"Make the challenge," I said.

Our little blue light flickered. Fifteen seconds passed.

"No reply, sir," reported the signalman.

I was just framing the words "Open fire", when the target altered course slightly and I recognised the silhouette as one of our trawlers. We swept past, raining silent curses upon it.

The night dragged on, but we were still in E-boat Alley. Although there had been no activity for some time, and risk of attack diminished as daylight approached, it was not safe to fall out from action stations. The next few hours seemed like days, but at last faint signs of dawn appeared, and we were able to relax. About eight o'clock I left the bridge after a six-teen-hour spell up there, and staggered down to my sea cabin. Ten minutes later the bell by my ear rang.

"Yes?"

"We're just passing a tug towing an oiler, sir; the latter looks in a pretty bad way."

I clambered wearily on to the bridge. The ship was a casualty from the night before, and the tug was heading for Lowestoft.

"He'll never make it."

As I spoke, the oiler took a heavy list to port. Men could be seen running along the upper deck, and a boat was turned out from its davits. At the same time a lamp flashed from the bridge—"Am abandoning . . ."

But the signal was never finished, for the ship's list to port increased rapidly until she gave a lurch and disappeared; in the bubbling, muddy waters the ship's boat rocked and tossed about, and men's heads popped up like currants in a bun. Fortunately the tug picked up all the survivors; and after we had dropped a buoy to mark the position of the wreck, we pressed on once more to rejoin the convoy; finally we arrived at Sheerness on a cold drizzly afternoon.

Although the convoy had lost three ships, later reports showed that several E-boats had been sunk and damaged, not only by the escorts but also by our own M.G.B.'s and Coastal Command aircraft who attacked them while they were return-ing to harbour at dawn.

It was one of the fiercest E-boat battles of the war, and the escorts received a special message of congratulation from the Admiralty. In *Verdun* we were not certain whether this in-cluded us, as our contribution to the firing had been exactly nil.

Another night that winter we were in the rear of a north-bound convoy, one ship of which we knew to be carrying an especially valuable cargo. At dusk there was a roar of aircraft engines to seaward. The guns trained round on the alarm bear-ing, and a few seconds later a Heinkel appeared.

"Open fire!"

We managed to get off one salvo fairly close to the enemy before it flew off in the mist right over the special ship in question, dropping two bombs. As darkness came down, the weather got worse, with heavy rain squalls reducing the visibility to a few hundred yards.

"Keep an eye on the special job," I told the signalman.

"She's dropping astern, sir."

At that moment the bell rang from the wireless office.

"Yes?"

"Signal from C.-in-C., sir—E-boat activity expected tonight."

"Very good."

I gazed anxiously astern: the other ship was practically out of sight, and we ourselves were only doing seven knots. It was blowing strongly now from the North East, and a short sharp sea had got up. I could not really believe that there would be any E-boats about in that weather, but one could never be quite certain.

"We can't leave this bird alone," I said, "though God knows what's the matter with him."

I turned *Verdun* round, and came up on the other ship's beam to seaward: we hailed her by loudspeaker, but there was no reply.

"Don't flash at her," I said, "or she'll probably answer with a ruddy great searchlight that'll attract every E-boat in the North Sea."

We took station ahead of the ship, and zig-zagged at about fifteen knots across her line of advance. The main convoy was by now out of sight ahead of us: however, all was comparatively well, it was merely a case of shepherding this straggler throughout the night. About midnight we came up to Smith's Knoll, a point on the convoy route where it was necessary to alter course. The weather had now got very much worse with blinding rainstorms and heavy squalls.

"Seen the buoy yet?" I asked.

"No, sir."

Visibility was now only a few hundred yards.

"We must have passed it by now," I said, "bring her round on to the new course." At that moment a particularly heavy squall came down, and we lost sight of our precious charge astern.

We never saw a sign of her again, but we spent the whole of a miserable night circling round searching for her: we were not

D

fitted with a surface radar set, and the Haisborough shoal and
other sandbanks were horribly close under our lee to the
Southwest, with no light buoys to mark them. We steamed
towards them as near as we dared.

"I'm damn well not going aground," I said, "even if she
has."

At daylight, a southbound convoy hove in sight.

"What-are-you-playing-at?" flashed the senior escort.

We described briefly our night's hide-and-seek among the
shoals, and another destroyer was sent to investigate to the
southward; eventually the merchant ship was discovered stuck
fast on a sandbank.

As far as I know she is still there.

Christmas, 1941, was not a very happy one. Those of us
who had been in China were especially sick at heart at the news
of the surrender of Hong Kong. On the East Coast, the weather
seemed to get worse every trip: on the northbound trip with the
ships in ballast, high out of the water with their propellers
thrashing away at about half-efficiency, the problem of
stragglers was ever present.

The rear escort had to decide whether to order such ships
into an intermediate port to await the next convoy—a step
unpopular with all concerned—or else to stand by them during
the night when danger of E-boat attack was likely. After
pottering along all one night with a straggler, we were not un-
amused to discover at daylight that its name was *Speedfast*!

Once north of the Humber, there was no danger of E-boat
attack, and as the war went on the danger of air attack gradually
diminished, though it was always possible. However, there were
plenty of problems to keep us busy. Approaching the Tees and
Tyne, when there was a strong westerly wind the industrial
haze from that area was often carried out to sea, so that at the
junction point (20 C Buoy, I shall never forget its number)
where some ships left to enter harbour, and others came out to
join up, there was always a fine schemozzle.

Thus the sea was a confused mass of ships barging about all
over the place, with sirens hooting and wheezing on all sides.
It was on just such an occasion, and we had just gone to action
stations in anticipation of the usual air attack, when Michael
Marwood appeared on the bridge.

"There's a fire broken out in the stewards' flat, sir." (The stewards' flat was next to the after magazine.)

My heart sank. We'd had enough of fires after the "do" at Rosyth.

"Well get cracking on it," was my reply. "Let me know what's happening."

Fire on board a ship is the most awful menace. If it is an electrical one, water is useless to put it out; at the same time foamites and pyrenes leave a shocking mess behind them. And the presence of ammunition does not exactly add to one's peace of mind. As the minutes passed, telephoned reports reached the bridge. The whole flat was full of smoke—Number One had gone down in the fire helmet . . . Any moment I expected the ship to blow up. At last the report was received: "Fire extinguished." Shortly afterwards, Number One appeared on the bridge, grinning all over.

"Rather funny, really, sir," he said. "When the stewards went up to action stations, they'd left the electric fire switched on. The leading steward had left his coat hanging over the fire and, with the roll of the ship, it must have fallen down and caught alight. Hell of a blaze when I got down there!"

The steward in question had the nerve to claim for compensation on the Admiralty for his burned coat. He got a monumental "blast" from me instead, for his stupidity!

However, we were not the only ship where accidents occurred. Shortly afterwards, we entered the Tyne with two other destroyers, and berthed alongside each other in the Tyne at Oslo Quay. One of the others, the *Westminster*, had a fine war record and little silhouettes of aircraft she had shot down and E-boats she had sunk were painted on every gunshield. Air attack was always a possibility, even in harbour, and in wartime ships always kept the armament loaded. By some mischance on this occasion, one of the *Westminster's* 4-inch guns was fired off into the blue. Hearing the report, I ran up on deck to see their Gunnery Officer, speechless with horror, gazing after the shell which had exploded in the distance somewhere over the busy docks. In the deathly silence that followed, a voice called out from *Verdun*.

"Nice work, Guns; now paint a tram on your —— gunshield!"

I nearly killed myself in Rosyth harbour when the ship was lying quite peacefully alongside. I was down in the wardroom having lunch, when all the lights went out due to a power cut or some such reason. Anyone familiar with the old "V and W" class destroyers will remember that the magazine was below the wardroom, but that the hatch down to the magazine was in the lobby outside under the ladder leading to the upper deck.

For some extraordinary reason the hatch had been left open just at that particular moment when I left the wardroom to go up on deck: it was very dark in the lobby but I knew my way about, and stepped confidently out towards the ladder: the next thing I knew I was halfway down the magazine hatch. By some miracle, I just put my hand out in time to catch the top of the coaming, and so saved myself from horrid injuries, or possibly even sudden death. But I got a very nasty shock, and felt the effects of it for several days.

Just about then, Toby Rodwell left the ship, and Lieutenant Terry, R.N.R., took over the job as Pilot. Terry was from West Australia; I can best describe him by saying he resembled in many ways the well-known Mr. Hardy of Laurel and Hardy fame. While he was not the world's greatest sailor, he was a decided asset to the wardroom and ship. I do not remember ever once seeing him depressed or downhearted.

One day in March, 1942, *Verdun* was with a northbound convoy just south of Flamborough when one of the merchant ships hoisted a flag signal which was not immediately familiar. "Have sick man aboard, please send doctor," announced the signalman, after quickly thumbing through his book.

Shortly afterwards our whaler was on its way with Doc Strang perched in the stern. A nasty choppy sea was running, and the coxswain of the whaler, for reasons best known to himself, chose to go to the windward side of the merchant ship. On *Verdun's* bridge we watched the doctor swinging perilously to and fro as he climbed aboard, and then disappeared below deck. A signal followed to the effect that the sick man had peritonitis, and an operation was essential within a few hours if his life was to be saved.

I thought quickly. The convoy was clear of E-boat Alley now, and danger of air attack was slight; there were also extra escorts with the convoy, of which I was the senior officer. I decided to take the sick man on board and proceed into the Tyne at best speed. I made the necessary signals; within a few minutes the whaler carrying the sick man was hoisted inboard, and *Verdun* set off for the Tyne. Doc Strang came up on the bridge with a serious expression.

"I give him about three or four hours, sir, at the most."

"Well, we'll have a stab at it. Ring on 25 knots, Sub."

It was blowing strongly from the North East, and *Verdun* began to pound with great "wumphs" into the head seas which shook the ship from end to end. Soon Doc Strang came up on the bridge again.

"I'm afraid you ought to ease down a little, sir," he said anxiously. "This bumping is just the worst thing for him. We'll have to accept the longer time at sea. It'll be touch and go in any case."

We reduced speed slightly but with an adverse tide, the Yorkshire coast crept by very slowly. A signal had been received from the Tyne that a boat would be waiting at the river entrance, but we soon realised that would be out of the question with the heavy seas that were now running. As we turned up towards the Tyne, Strang came up on the bridge again.

"How much longer, sir? It's a question of minutes almost."

I was looking even more anxiously at the entrance to the Tyne. Heavy seas were dashing against the breakwater, inside of which was flat calm. There was a wreck dangerous to navigation sunk plumb in the entrance, and ships were ordered to pass it at slow speed. It was going to be pretty tricky getting in; we would need to do it at a fair speed to keep control of the ship at the instant of passing from the heavy beam-on swell outside the breakwater to the dead flat water inside.

With a silent prayer to the Almighty, I increased speed to 20 knots and we shot in past the breakwater. The moment that the bows entered the calm water, the stern was swung violently round by the swell outside, and I had to stop the port engine and go astern on it to prevent us running on to the north bank under Tynemouth.

Even so, we passed the wrong side of a buoy, but by the grace of God there was enough water, and we sailed on up the river at a cracking pace. Indignant toots from ferries and other shipping were ignored as we headed into Oslo Quay, where an ambulance was waiting on the jetty. We secured alongside, and the gangway was run out. A Naval staff car was there, and by one of those curious coincidences so difficult to explain (particularly to disbelieving wives), the driver was the blonde Wren Constance whom I had met when *Guillemot* was refitting in Sunderland.

"Bring 'em back alive, that's the stuff," she said.

The forward gun's crew were much impressed.

"Only bin 'ere five minutes and the skipper's got off already," one of them was heard to murmur.

The sick man was hurried ashore, and within ten minutes of our arrival alongside, we went astern out into the river again, and downstream at a more sedate pace to rejoin the convoy. On return to Rosyth a few days later, we heard the operation had been successful and the man's life saved.

I sent for Doc Strang and told him the good news.

"You London doctors are simply wonderful," I said.

"Yes, sir," said Doc Strang modestly.

We drank to the old seaman's speedy recovery: it seemed as appropriate a toast as any.

When the better weather came along in the spring, an effort was always made whilst on passage north to contact one of the Yorkshire fishing trawlers off Flamborough or Whitby. The drill was that on sighting a trawler conveniently close, the junior escort signalled the senior: "Request permission to investigate suspicious craft." The reply was invariably in the affirmative.

The escort then closed the trawler and received baskets of fresh fish in exchange for—well, the Captain, if he was wise, did not inquire too closely as to the contents of the tins that were passed back into the trawler. On rejoining convoy, the escort signalled: "Craft proved friendly. Request pleasure of your company at lunch on return to harbour." The reply to that was invariably in the affirmative too.

In the summer months, E-boat torpedo activity was restricted somewhat, but they nipped over now and then to lay mines in the Tramlines, as did also their aircraft. The score of ships sunk by mines mounted despite all our efforts, and there were dozens of these stumbling blocks between Humber and Thames. To have run into one of them could hardly have failed to sink the ship.

It was in this connection that I had two astonishing experiences of premonition—in exactly the same manner as I had on *Guillemot's* first trip. One summer evening, *Verdun* was escorting a convoy of about thirty ships: the latter were ambling along at seven knots, in two columns as usual, a few hundred yards apart.

The convoy always proceeded in two columns inside the swept channel, which was none too wide. The escorts were stationed ahead and astern of the convoy and also on either flank. The latter position could be uncomfortable. If the ships in the convoy got rather off course, and "edged over in the bed" one was then obliged to squeeze unpleasantly close to the dangers on the outside.

On this occasion, *Verdun* was on the port flank of the convoy. It was just before sunset, and I had left the bridge to get a few minutes' rest in my sea cabin by the wheelhouse. The sea was flat calm and visibility moderate, an ideal night for an E-boat attack. I was lying on my bunk, wondering what particular horrors the night would bring forth, and I suppose I must have closed my eyes.

"Get up on the bridge!"

I shot up in my bunk, fully alert at once. I could have sworn I heard a voice, but my cabin was empty. Empty, that is, except for a feeling of intense danger. A glance at my watch showed I had only dozed off for a few minutes, but instantly I knew something was wrong. In a flash I was out of the door and running up the ladder on to the bridge.

"Hard-a-starboard!"

I shouted down to the helmsman the instant that I reached the compass platform. For a quick glance ahead had shown me a wreck-buoy marking a dangerous wreck half a cable away and dead in our course. From the chart table, tucked away in the corner of the bridge, the scared faces of the Officer of the Watch and the signalman looked up at me like Walt Disney rabbits. They had been discussing some signal that had just come in, and heaven only knows whether the buoy would have been spotted had I not appeared in the nick of time! Another half minute and it would have been too late. That premonition of danger was so strong as to be absolutely unmistakable and a few months later, very nearly in the same spot in the North Sea, I experienced it again. The second time it was even more remarkable.

We were steaming northwards then on the same route with a smaller convoy of only eleven ships. The escorts were the destroyers *Vivien* and *Verdun*. It needed no great mathematician to realise that the party totalled thirteen. In *Verdun* we had just received a signal to the effect that we would dock for our annual refit on completion of the trip at Rosyth. As refit obviously included a spot of leave everyone on board was in high spirits.

All day, then, after leaving the Thames estuary, the convoy plodded along at seven knots; the ships were in ballast high out of the water, with propellers thrashing and splashing away. The day passed quietly, but about four o'clock we received a signal from a trawler on patrol near a certain buoy some miles ahead of us to the effect that an enemy aircraft had been seen to drop two mines in the sea nearby. The exact position could not be given, and of course the convoy was not going to be deterred by the small matter of a couple of mines somewhere ahead. The whole sea was strewn with them anyhow, and two more did not make much difference. So we just went on as usual, keeping inside the swept channel reported clear by our minesweepers.

As we approached the danger area, the *Vivien*, who was the senior escort, signalled the convoy to close the distance between the columns. This obviously lessened the risk of passing over the position of either mine, which we guessed were either magnetic or acoustic ones. We in *Verdun* were in rear of the convoy and were thus thirteenth ship. The Officer of the Watch, Stan Terry, rubbed the fact well home.

"Thirteenth and last ship," he remarked to everyone on the bridge, "on our last convoy before refit, too. Funny if we bought it, wouldn't it?"

"Thanks a lot," I said, but I had an awful feeling that it was just the sort of thing that would happen.

With fingers crossed, we watched the ships ahead pass the danger area safely one by one. First the *Vivien*, then the

Commodore's ship, then the next . . . then the next . . . There was dead silence on the bridge as we counted. Six . . . seven . . . eight . . . Suddenly the collier ahead of us, which was of course the twelfth ship in the line, started to slow down, and then stopped. A lamp flickered from her bridge. "Minor engine defect. Will be delayed a few minutes."

At the same time she yawed slightly out of the line to starboard. As there was no point in *Verdun* hanging around in the danger area, I altered course to pass under the collier's stern, and we steamed past: then we eased down to keep an eye on her. And then, as before, an overwhelming premonition of danger passed through my mind quite suddenly. I simply knew exactly what was going to happen.

"Away sea boat's crew! Man the sea boat!"

A voice rapped out the order: my own voice, though it did not seem to me that I had actually spoken. In two minutes the boat was manned and lowered to the waterline, ready to slip.

"All ready, sir."

As the Coxswain sang out from the boat there was a heavy explosion astern. The collier listed over, and sank before she had time to turn her lifeboat out. But ours was by then in the water and picked up every man.

I have often thought about that twist of Fate that caused the collier's engine failure at that vital moment, which led to her being sunk and not *Verdun*: and far more vividly do I recall the intensity of that premonition of danger on both those occasions out at sea.

CHAPTER IX

STAND EASY AND THE SECOND HALF

OUR REFIT in August took place at Grangemouth. Before the ship's company went on leave, I had occasion to clear lower deck to say a few words about this and that. I kept the best item to the last.

"I have just been to see Captain (D)," I said, "and he has asked me to tell you that he is very pleased with *Verdun*. In this last year, we are the only destroyer in the flotilla who has never failed to escort the convoy allotted to her."

It was quite true. Out of some seventy occasions of being ordered to sail, only once had we not sailed at the time ordered: the single exception was when a minor defect delayed the ship by about an hour, but we then sailed and caught the convoy up before it had left the Forth.

A very satisfactory record, for which full credit was due to Chiefee Seabrook and his staff: they worked like niggers to keep the twenty-five-year-old ship running. I was very pleased later to get Seabrook a Mention in Despatches for this record.

During the refit, there were several changes in the wardroom. One of them was the Gunner: his relief was to be a Lieutenant R.N.V.R. I viewed the prospective change without enthusiasm. I envisaged in my mind's eye a very young, earnest, and rather dull youth. When I saw John Heywood for the first time, I realised my estimate could not have been wider of the mark. He was older than myself, very plump, bald as an egg, with twinkling eyes and a rubicund complexion. He looked exactly like a City stockbroker.

"What was your line in life outside?" I asked.

"A stockbroker, sir—in the City."

Then I really did laugh: I was still doing so half an hour later. Heywood's penchant for purple stories was well in accordance with the highest City standards.

Doc Strang's relief was another V.R. type, by name Yellow-lees, a young man from Glasgow. A trifle dour in his personal appearance, he nevertheless had a keen sense of humour, and was an excellent foil for Heywood. Indeed, I do not think it would have been possible to have found in the whole of the Navy a destroyer wardroom as cheerful as the *Verdun's* just then; and if at times they might have overstepped the mark—well, one needed every possible ounce of humour to compete with life on the East Coast convoys in winter time.

I suppose it is not a very common occurrence for the Commanding Officer of a ship, returning aboard late at night, to find a bicycle in his bunk: doubtless it was my own fault for hinting that to convey my bicycle down the hatch would be an impossible feat. After I had looked at the thing bent into a Picasso tangle on my bunk, I went down into the wardroom; there was an air of hushed expectancy, a ring of grinning faces like a lot of children waiting for father's re-action to the booby-trap.

"Ha! Ha!" I said, "ha-bloody-ha! I suppose you think you're all frightfully funny."

There were roars of delight all round the wardroom.

"So glad you didn't mind, sir," said the Pilot, giving me a drink, "we just wondered afterwards——"

"—Mind?" I said, "Good Heavens, no—damn funny joke. Ha! Ha! Now tell me all about it."

They explained at great length how they had found my bicycle on the jetty; the difficulty they had had getting it over the gangway; how the Pilot had fallen over twice carrying it along the upper deck; and finally the tremendous struggle they had had to get it through the hatch and down the ladder.

"Took us hours, sir," said Guns.

"'Fraid we've rather bent it about, sir," said the Pilot.

"We wanted to be quite sure you wouldn't lose it, sir," added the Doc.

They had me in stitches, I was rolling about in my chair. Eventually I dried my eyes.

"And now," I said, "you can just take it right back where you found it—becaue it's not my bike at all!"

The real owner (Chief in another ship) cut up pretty rough next day when he discovered the truth: but then, of course, some fellows have no sense of humour.

Our refit passed only too quickly and October, 1942, saw *Verdun* back on the Tramlines again: and we needed all the happiest memories possible to help us face the prospect of another winter at sea.

Even now I shiver when I think of some of those nights, plugging along into the teeth of a north-easter through the Wold Channel, with the Haisborough sandbanks close to starboard and the Norfolk coast equally adjacent to port, with the convoy in ballast and almost stationary against wind and tide. One night three ships ran ashore in succession: the leader was carrying vital machine tools to open up a factory in Australia. Not a very bright start to such a long trip.

The snag about the bridge of a destroyer like *Verdun* was that there was so little room to move about, particularly when there were three or four other fellows on the bridge as well. You could not move more than a pace or two without bumping into someone or something, so most of the time you just had to stay put in one position. During those long winter nights, therefore, to keep warm was hard enough, but to keep awake was even harder. It was sheer agony at times. Perhaps I used to overdo it: if so, it was not because I did not rely on the Officers of the Watch, but because my greatest bête-noire was the thought of not being on the bridge if any sudden disaster overtook us. But often after long spells up there at night, my brain became so numb with fatigue and cold that it became a positive effort to write out a signal, or make a sudden decision.

However, after my long experience on the coast I had acquired an absolute "mental map" of the route. I knew every course to steer, and every buoy almost by its Christian name— at least until one night that winter when I was caught napping.

We had left the Thames as usual at daylight, made our rendezvous with the convoy off the Nore, had our usual "confab" with the Commodore in the leading ship by loud hailer, mustered the convoy according to the list, and settled down to plug along northward. It was a moonlight period— luckily for us—and blowing fairly hard which lessened the chances of E-boat attack. We passed number five buoy which was about due east of Yarmouth at dusk, and steered north- wards for Smith's Knoll. Just about the time we were due to come up to it——

"Flashing light right ahead, sir," reported the signalman.

"Very good."

I gazed at it, mentally registered the number of flashes, and then instinctively I knew something was wrong.

"That's not Smith's Knoll buoy," I said to the Pilot "that light's flashing every five seconds. Smith's Knoll is two flashes every ten."

"Yes, sir."

We checked it again. It was definitely one every five.

"You're sure it hasn't been altered?" I asked.

"Yes, sir."

Fortunately for us there was a wreck with a green flashing buoy not far from Smiths' Knoll.

"Well, there's the wreck anyhow," I said, "we must be in the right place. Smith's Knoll must have gone wrong."

We altered course to the westward and led the convoy round: a glance at the stars showed we were heading roughly in the right direction anyway. The next buoy was five miles ahead, and in due course it was spotted by the lookout. I watched it like a hawk. It was not flashing as it should have been. I became a bit uneasy.

"Hey, something queer's going on. Are you *sure* these buoys have not been altered?"

"Quite sure, sir."

From the next buoy up to Sheringham the course was almost due west: there was a succession of wrecks along the route all marked by green flashing buoys; these were duly sighted and on this occasion, anyhow, I was glad to have that melancholy avenue of navigational aids. Off Sheringham, we had to make another large alteration of course again to the northward: Sheringham buoy was a well-known milestone on the route, and had the added advantage of having a bell on it. As we approached it on this particular night——

"This damn thing's different, too," I said angrily, "steer close to it and listen for the bell."

We heard the bell all right, and I brought the ship round to the northerly course. Just then the Pilot came up on the bridge: in the darkness I could not see his face, but it should have been beetroot red.

"I'm terribly sorry, sir," he said, "but I've just found this

Notice to Mariners. Ten of the buoys' lights were changed during daylight today in this area."

It was a move to try and fox the enemy: for the fact that it had foxed us as well, I could only hold myself to blame. It was part of the Pilot's job to correct the charts, of course, and he received from me a severe raspberry for being adrift on that occasion: but at the same time it was my responsibility, and a good kick in the pants for thinking I knew everything about the job. I did not, however, consider it neccessary to mention the affair in my convoy report.

At that time there was a great flap on about reducing top weight in destroyers; more and more guns, radar sets and other gadgets, were being fitted as time went on, and it suddenly dawned on some genius that the ships might be getting a bit top heavy. Inclining experiments were carried out in harbour which caused a great deal of inconvenience, and which the ignorant, like myself, thought all very unnecessary. Once again, I was due for a nasty shock.

This time it was on a southbound convoy and also in the Wold Channel area. A strong north-easterly gale was plumb on our port beam, and we were all rolling uncomfortably. During our refit a new radar set had been fitted high up in *Verdun's* superstructure, and there was no doubt we were rolling more than usual on this particular occasion. For some reason or other the convoy's speed came down to an absolute crawl, which further aggravated the rolling. In *Verdun*, stationed astern of the convoy, we were reduced to Slow Both during the middle watch—sticky moments always occurred in the middle, just to make them stickier—and suddenly we gave the most frightening lurch to starboard. I leapt to the voicepipe.

"Half ahead together—one five oh revolutions."

For what seemed eternity, but was probably only a couple of seconds, I thought we were going to roll right over. Then the ship righted herself, and we sped through the convoy like a dog through a herd of sheep. In a short space of time we were up to the leading escort, *Westminster*.

"What-brings-you-here?" she winked.

I explained briefly. At daylight the gale eased and when *Verdun* returned to round up the scattered convoy, one ship was missing. We searched for miles astern along the route, but not a sign was there to be seen. Not a man, not a spar was ever seen of her again; she may have been mined, but I am convinced that she did what we were within an inch of doing—rolled right over and disappeared for ever.

At that time many merchant ships had a winch fitted aft with a wire and small barrage balloon attached. The great idea was to fly the balloon about two hundred feet up to deter low-flying aircraft. Sometimes when a ship was sunk for whatever reason, the wire would remain connected, and prove a perfect marker to the ship out of sight below water. So "balloon marks the spot" was frequently signalled to the shore authorities at the end of a casualty report.

It was nearly made on *Verdun's* behalf once, entirely due to my stupidity. A ship flying its balloon was mined in daylight and sank at once. We closed the position and stopped to lower our whaler to collect survivors. In a moment of carelessness, coupled with anxiety, I had stopped *Verdun* to tideward of the position where the ship had just disappeared. A few minutes later, while our whaler was away picking up men in the water, I looked aft from the bridge, and saw the wire under our port side amidships, and the balloon being pulled down into our funnels. We had drifted down beam on on top of the sunken ship!

"Cut that wire, for God's sake!" I shouted.

Chief Stoker Ranger was on the upper deck. He looked up and realised the situation in a flash. I have never seen a man move quicker. Leaping to the bulkhead, he seized an axe and cut the wire. The balloon, filled with hydrogen, sailed away rapidly out of sight. In another few seconds it would have been drawn down on to our funnel and ignited. Ranger's quick action had saved us. It was a typical example of discipline, alertness of mind and resource—all those qualities, in fact, that Naval training endeavours to teach a man.

On the bridge I was still shaking all over. For a ghastly moment I thought *Verdun* was stuck there for ever, jammed on top of the wreck like a butterfly pinned on a collecting board. Fortunately, the sunken ship must have heeled over on the sea bottom, and we drifted clear. But it was an unpleasant few minutes, and another typical example also of how a momentary lapse on a Captain's part can put a ship in deadly hazard.

But such heart-attacks, once they were over, were best forgotten: life in Rosyth was far too gay to worry about the "might have been" memories at sea.

One day in March, 1943, *Verdun* came into harbour about six o'clock in the evening. We had spent the previous night at anchor down at the convoy anchorage at Methil: normally such a duty was not too arduous, and although I always slept in my sea cabin on such an occasion, I had taken the opportunity to sleep in pyjamas, instead of being fully dressed as at sea. However, some trouble of sorts had occurred during the night: I had been called on the bridge at short notice with just time to whip a scarf and uniform on over my pyjamas, and so I had remained all day. There had been no real opportunity, nor actual need for me to dress properly: I looked forward to a bath and proper change on arrival at Rosyth. We berthed alongside the *Wolsey*, whose skipper Tim Taylor was a crony of mine. As I gave the order to ring off the engines, he called over from his ship.

"Come over and have a nip."

"Thanks very much—later on, though. I must change first."

"Ah, rot—come on over now down to my cabin."

"I'm still in my sea rig——"

"—Come on over, man."

So over I went down to his cabin: there was just the pair of us, and we yarned away talking "shop". One drink was followed by the other half, and then there was a knock on the door. It was one of the *Wolsey's* officers.

"Would you care to come down to the wardroom, sir?" he said to Tim Taylor, "we have a few guests on board."

"Thanks very much—come on, Bill."

"I can't in this rig, man."

"Come on!"

There was no arguing with Tim, and anyhow we were all friends—they would quite understand. They all knew I had just come in from sea, and as long as I kept fairly still, nobody would know that I was not just in uniform with a scarf on instead of a tie and collar. There were several of the officers' wives aboard, plus a Wren or two, and we were all chatting away merrily when I saw one of the girls gazing with some amazement at my feet. I looked down and saw to my horror a small portion of pyjama trouser protruding. I tried to hide it, but too late.

"Look, everyone!" chortled the delighted girl, "Bill's come here in his pyjamas!"

Apologies and explanations were useless. I never lived it down. For some time afterwards I was greeted with—"Got your pyjamas on, Bill?"—when I went to cocktail parties.

As the spring of 1943 came along, enemy action eased off slightly: but the whole atmosphere of the East Coast convoys was one of standing by for action. Although on many a trip nothing happened, we also had to be ready for anything. One of the great dangers for the ship's company was boredom: at sea, day after day and night after night, they would close up on watch or at Action Stations, and nothing would happen—but when something did, it happened quickly and the danger was to be caught napping.

But at the end of each trip, it was a very satisfying sight to see the convoy entering harbour: it was something accomplished, something done. I never failed to get a thrill out of it. In *Verdun* we had a special flag of our own, not found in the official signal books. I cannot remember how we acquired it—probably just as well—but it was a large white flag with a broad green border. In the middle was a lovely glass of brown stout with a foamy white top, and underneath, in bright red letters, the words "Guiness is good for you!"

At the end of a particularly tough trip, when we had had an exasperating struggle with the enemy or the weather, or possibly both, we used to hoist that flag just before arrival in the Thames. Then we would turn and steam back past the line of ships in convoy. From every bridge would come a cheery wave of the hand, or a toot-toot on the siren, or a signal flash: "Meet you ashore for one tonight."

In April we were sent to Sheerness to join up with the 21st Flotilla, but we had not been there long when we had special orders to sail to Portsmouth. This was, indeed, a change of air from Rosyth, and an even fresher blow was to come. *Verdun* was ordered to escort the French battleship *Courbet* in tow of two tugs up to the Clyde.

The trip up to the Clyde was interesting but uneventful. We were ordered to return northabout to Rosyth at once.

"We are seeing the world," I said to Stan Terry, "I trust we have the necessary charts—and that they are corrected up to date also."

After passing Ailsa Craig, we had an extraordinary experience. We were steering a westerly course between the North of Ireland and the Mull of Kintyre at fifteen knots; it was a fair day, with only a very slight sea. I left the bridge to get a few hours sleep before what I knew would be a tricky passage through the Minches in the dark, and had just shut my eyes when there was an appalling bang; the ship shuddered as though we had run slap into a vertical cliff. At once the thought "Collision!" flashed through my mind. I ran up on the bridge, arriving there just as the second "thud" occurred. I leapt to the voice-pipe.

"Slow both!"

There was not a ship in sight, but coming at us from right ahead in a most alarming way was a succession of enormous Atlantic rollers: luckily they were absolutely dead ahead, and the immediate reduction of speed saved us from damage. In a few minutes the sea was almost flat calm again. It may be a natural occurrence in that narrow neck of water, but it certainly gave us a nasty fright. It was not the only one we were to have that trip.

By the time we reached Skerryvore, and turned almost due north, the outlook was most depressing. Visibility was very much reduced, and the trip up the Minches in the dark an absolute nightmare. It was a dark, misty, moonless night, and although we requested two lights to be lit for us on the West coast, we only sighted one of them for a few minutes on Vaternish Point. From there we had a fifteen mile run, passing fairly close to an unlit, unfamiliar, and rocky coast all the way till we came to the gap between it and the little island of Trodday, lying less than a mile off shore. I do not think I have ever had such an agonising trip as that one. A lighted buoy had been laid close to the westward of the gap, and with straining eyes the signalman and I peered anxiously through the gloom for it, while Number One concentrated on the chart, timing the ship's run and giving me the courses.

"Lighted buoy fine on starboard bow, sir!"

Such relief as I felt vanished at once when a second report followed close on the heels of the first.

"Land right ahead, sir!"

My heart nearly stopped beating. I whipped up my glasses, and saw a black mass dead ahead. But luckily I soon saw it was a trawler or some small ship stern on, and steering the same course; she had no lights, and as we watched, she altered to starboard for the gap between mainland and Troddy a mile or so ahead. There was only one thing to do, and that was to beat her to the gap.

It was an extraordinary race. To starboard and most uncomfortably close, the mainland hung over our head like some monster waiting to pounce; to port, just visible through the gloom was the island, with the sea breaking over it in angry fashion; to port, also, and literally only a few yards off was the trawler, pudging along obviously quite unconscious of our presence. Had I sounded our siren, or flashed at her, I was sure she would have altered across our bows in panic or done something equally silly: so I just slammed on speed and raced past.

"I bet that gave their O.O.W. a shock," chuckled Number One.

"Teach him to keep his eyes open," I growled.

Once safely through the gap, there was a straight run across to Cape Wrath. I nipped down to my sea cabin, and seemingly had only just closed my eyes, when the bell rang.

"Cape Wrath in sight, sir, and my God, it looks it too, sir," said Guns.

He did not need to tell me. The *Verdun* was already rolling heavily as we came clear of the lee of the Isle of Lewis, and got the full benefit of a westerly gale on our port beam. Tremendous seas were pounding themselves to pieces against the Cape, and as we rounded it, we were nastily pooped by a stern sea.

"Twenty knots," I said.

Then followed a most exhilarating run along the North Coast of Scotland in bright sunshine with a strong following wind and sea.

"On the crest of the wave," I remarked to Number One.

"In every way, sir," he replied, "a signal has just come through for us to boiler clean on arrival."

"I did a spot of quick calculation on the chart.

"We'll have to steam to make it tonight," I said.

At that time there were only two decent trains south from Edinburgh per day, one about nine a.m. and the other about nine p.m. As most of the ship's company lived in the South of England, it was most desirable for us to get in in time to catch the night train. We increased speed, and all that day sped down the East coast; but with the perversity of Fate, a strong southerly wind arose and we were bucking into a nasty choppy head sea all the way.

As we reached May Island, and turned into the calmer water of the Firth of Forth, I looked down from the bridge and saw the upper deck crowded with men, all ready in their shore-going rig. A row of anxious faces were looking up at the bridge. It was never particularly pleasant going up to Rosyth in the dark, and especially so when the visibility was only moderate. But my heart was warmed by the sight of those men waiting there, literally looking up to me; I knew that twelve precious hours of leave depended on my judgment.

"Will we make it, sir?" asked Number One, as he came up on the bridge.

"We're going to have a damn good try," I said, "ring on twenty-five knots."

The order was repeated almost before I had finished speaking. The Officer of the Watch was going on leave also.

"Tell the Chief to give her all he's got," I added. (For normal cruising only two boilers were lit out of the three; thus our maximum speed just then was about twenty-five, or a bit more.)

Like the echo of those hundred anxious hearts beating, the *Verdun* throbbed her way up the Firth, through the boom gates at Inchkeith and Oxcars, and finally glided to a standstill under the great bridge. Here the libertymen piled into a boat provided by the dockyard; in less than no time they were landed at South Queensferry, and running up the two hundred and-something steps to the railway station. We could just see them in the distance like a crowd of ants.

"Cor!" chuckled the signalman from his telescope, "look at Tubby—'e'll never make it!"

One figure was toiling slowly upwards a long way behind

the others; but he staggered out of sight onto the station, just as the southbound train from Inverkeithing to Edinburgh thundered over the great bridge above our heads, and drew up at the platform. I derived peculiar satisfaction from that little affair. The men had never let me down, and for once, perhaps, I had been able to return the compliment.

In May, 1943, I left *Verdun* after nearly two years in command. I was very sorry to do so. It is never easy to compare ships in my own personal experience, when life in each one of them has been such good value, but *Verdun* tops my list by a short head. I number among my proudest possessions two presents I was given after leaving her: a silver salver from the ship's company, and a decanter from the wardroom.

In leaving *Verdun*, I also left the East Coast convoys after nearly three years on the job. Those were the most worthwhile years of my whole time at sea: every trip was interesting, and at times very exciting, and the safe arrival of each convoy in harbour a definite contribution to the war effort. Both in *Guillemot* and *Verdun* I had complete confidence in my ship and those on board. I have never pretended to be anything but a perfectly ordinary fellow; I made many mistakes, but I did my best, and I always asked for God's guidance to help me do so.

I can only add that I took those two ships *Guillemot* and *Verdun* out to sea on over one hundred and fifty occasions: we encountered every sort of danger and witnessed every sort of disaster: gales and fog, bombs and mines, collisions and grounding—the whole lot of them. Yet in all those trips in *Guillemot* and *Verdun*, not one man was ever killed or wounded, and neither ship suffered the slightest damage whatever.

I think a great deal about those trips, and especially so in winter time. I remember so vividly the two lines of ships, butting along steadily through the darkness, come hell or high water, for five and a half years—until the light of victory dawned.

Even more vividly do I remember, with admiration and humble pride, such men as the Chief Engineer of one of those ships. We fished him out of the water with two others only, from a crew of twenty; their ship had been mined, and it sank almost before the sound of the explosion had died away. Aged over sixty, with a broken leg and other injuries, his only thought was to get to sea again.

"I'll be back soon," he said, as we put him ashore at Rosyth, "they'll no' get me down."

They'll no' get me down. . . .

And most vividly of all do I remember those two ships of mine, *Guillemot* and *Verdun*, steaming steadily into harbour on over a hundred and fifty occasions, into Sheerness and Harwich, Humber and Tyne, up the Firth of Forth and under the great bridge, guided there in safety by the hand of God.

PART THREE

PATROLLING TO ATTACK

Chapter X

A NEW TOY

"A NEW TOY beginning with 'U'," said the voice on the phone.

"Building?" I asked.

"Yes, and not far from you. Same type as your last job."

"Goody-goody!"

"Think of an overcoat," added the voice, and rang off.

And so, after a pleasant leave in perfect summer weather, I went off to take over command of H.M.S. *Ulster*, a brand new "Fleet" Class destroyer, building at Swan Hunter's yard at Wallsend-on-Tyne. She was about 2,000 tons and 365 feet in length—at first sight she looked like a battleship compared with *Verdun*. Her complement was 225; for armament she had four 4.7-inch guns, eight torpedo tubes, a power-operated double-barrelled Bofors, and four pairs of power-worked Oerlikons.

Lieutenant Trevor Rushworth was First Lieutenant. I had known him in the same capacity in *Versatile* on the East Coast. He was a first-class officer, a good messmate and most conscientious in dealing with all the hundred-and-one problems facing the Executive Officer of a large destroyer. Lieutenant (E) "Nigger" Williamson, D.S.C., was the Chief, a great, hearty Devonian, and as good a Chief and shipmate as one could ever wish for in a destroyer.

As the building of the ship progressed, the other officers joined; the R.N. officers were Gunner J. A. Fallwell and Sub-Lieutenant John Bostock, and three young R.N.V.R. officers: Andrew Gray, D.S.C., R. Birtwistle, and J. Rutherford. Last, but by no means least, was our genial redfaced Irish Doc, William Johnston. He always reminded me of the Glaxo baby portrayed in the advertisements of that famous firm. They were a very good wardroom, and tackled their various jobs with energy and enthusiasm.

With a ship's company of over two hundred, it took me some time to size them up; there was the usual good backbone of experienced Service types, among them Coxswain Landles who had also been in *Versatile*; the Chief Boatswain's Mate, Turner, a quiet type, but a very good seaman; the Chief ERA, Dear by name, who had a tremendous responsibility with all the new machinery under his watchful eye; and the two senior Gunnery and Torpedo ratings, P.O. Flint and Chief P.O. Hunt respectively. There was also a very large number of young and inexperienced ratings with no sea time whatsoever; most of them turned out well, though as usual there were the individual "crows".

Once again I had the fun of watching a new ship being built, and of taking her over after her trials, when I signed a receipt for "One destroyer", which is not a thing one does every day. I have that receipt still. We had a small commissioning party on the 21st June, for which my wife and her mother came over from Keswick, with a black kitten from our home. This was christened "Geordie", but on second thoughts it was obvious that error had crept in, and the name was changed to "Georgina", and then "Georgia". She had a variety of adventures denied to the ordinary stay-at-home cat!

On the 25th of June the *Ulster* left Swan Hunter's yard for the last time after trials, bound for active service; crowds of workmen gave us a cheer as we left, and the firm's pilot who took her down as far as the breakwater shook my hand warmly.

"All the best, sir," he whispered, "don't worry, you'll be O.K.—you've got a nice ship, sir."

We did a full-power trial on passage up to Rosyth; by a stroke of luck we met the *Verdun* southward bound with a convoy, and exchanged signals while some way off. Proud of my new toy, I altered course to pass fairly close to *Verdun*, and at that critical moment the *Ulster's* steering gear chose to break down! We found ourselves heading straight for *Verdun*, and for a ghastly few seconds I foresaw the most terrible collision between my brand new command and my old one, but luckily the defect was remedied in time, and we swept past with much waving and signalling. But what the crew in *Verdun* thought I was playing at, I cannot imagine. After a few days in Rosyth, my friend Roy Exton came aboard and asked if we could give him a lift to Scapa. That was easily fixed, and he brought his gear aboard a few minutes before sailing.

"By Jove, you've got a fine ship," he exclaimed, "and what a picture she is now, brand new. Not a scratch anywhere."

He had hardly finished speaking when there was a terrific bump up forward, and we both ran out on deck. As I looked at the ship's bows, my language was regrettable but, under the circumstances, excusable. *Ulster* had berthed in a corner with her stem right up close to the dockyard wall; as it happened, while Roy and I were talking in my cabin, an over-zealous artificer down below, in testing the main engines before sailing, had opened the main manœuvring valve a fraction of an inch. The puff of high pressure steam that had slipped through was enough to turn the turbines, and hence the propellers, for just a kick; unfortunately this was enough to push the ship forward a few feet, parting some wires, and bashing the stem into the wall. No serious damage was done, but the ship's towing bullring right forward was bent upwards like a girl's retrousse nose.

"Just my luck," I growled; "when we get to Scapa, all the chaps will say—Typical of Donald; give him a new toy and he bashes it about straight away."

I was rather peeved about it, and even more so the next morning; visibility had decreased when we arrived off Duncansby Head, and a slight gyro error, which passed unnoticed for some minutes, caused us to miss the southern entrance to Scapa. We steamed on too far to the eastward and when visibility cleared we suddenly found ourselves heading for the narrow gap on the east side of the island through which Prien, the German submarine ace, had entered to sink the *Royal Oak* nearly four years previously. Feeling no end of an ass, I turned the ship round, and we eventually entered by Switha gate as expected; but luckily nobody ashore had seen anything.

We spent three weeks at Scapa working up. It was a tremendous job trying to get a brand new ship with a very raw crew into any sort of efficiency. We went through every sort of exercise at sea, and many in harbour; in addition, many administrative details had to be sorted out. We had, however, our lighter moments.

Being the newest ship in company and general dogsbody we

were given the worst berth in harbour, miles away from anywhere, down in the appropriately-named Gutter Sound. However, this was the nearest berth to the hospital ship *Isle of
Jersey*, where Roy Exton had gone to stay for a few days with
a Surgeon-Lieutenant Salmon. There were some very charming nurses on board *Isle of Jersey*, and Roy brought some on
board *Ulster* one evening. This introduction resulted in some
very pleasant parties, and greatly offset the monotony of the
working-up period.

After *Ulster* had been at Scapa for some time, I was invited to
dine with some other C.O.s aboard the depot ship *Tyne* with
the Admiral Commanding Destroyers, Rear Admiral Glennie.

"I've asked some Wren officers along," remarked the
Admiral genially, as I arrived in his cabin. "I don't suppose
you've seen a feminine face for weeks, have you?"

"Almost forgotten what they look like, sir," I replied—
a party of nurses had had lunch in *Ulster* that afternoon.

However, we did not do anything so rash the next day when
we were duty destroyer, which was just as well; for as we were
sitting down to dinner a signal arrived—

"Sail forthwith. Further orders follow."

We left our dinner to get cold.

"Stand by for action," I said to Number One.

Actually it was nothing very drastic, and it proved a very
welcome break for us; the escorting destroyer of a small troopship *Ben Machree*, en route to the Faroes, had developed engine
trouble, and was returning to harbour, so *Ulster* was ordered to
take her place. At the time we cursed heartily as we raced into
the teeth of a strong westerly to pick up *Ben Machree* twenty
miles or so to the northwestward of Scapa, but like so many
things, it turned out much better than we anticipated.

Next morning the two islands Suderoe and Sandoe rose out
of the mist ahead like the fangs of a gigantic wolf. Keeping a
respectable distance until we had pinpointed our position, we
then skirted the north-eastern end of Sandoe, and led the *Ben
Machree* into the gap between it and the next island, Stromoe.
There was an anti-submarine minefield laid in this gap, with
the mines laid at such a depth that we could pass over with
safety, but all the same I kept my fingers crossed until we were
clear. Our ultimate destination was Thorshavn, the capital of

the group of islands, but in the meanwhile the *Ben Machree*
had to exchange army reliefs at some of the small outlying
harbours, and we spent an interesting morning in and around
the islands.

"Cripes, look at that!" I exclaimed.

Towering black cliffs rose up vertically from the sea in shapes
and proportions that were fantastic, indeed almost terrifying,
to behold. Ant-like we proceeded on our way, and at noon
emerged on the west coast of Stromoe through a gap which
gave me the impression of having taken the ship through a
railway tunnel. The spectacle of these cliffs was enhanced by
the knowledge that the Faroes themselves were just specks in
the vast wastes of the Atlantic. At the end of one fjord, close to
a positive Cleopatra's Needle of rock, a sizeable river ended its
career with a lighthearted leap of several hundred feet into the
sea.

We turned our backs on the Atlantic at Vaago Fjord and
steamed serenely into its lee; in peaceful calm, basking in an
unexpected but welcome burst of midday sunshine, we watched
the Faroese farmers haymaking on the almost vertical fields
above. The war just then seemed a million miles away. That
evening we returned to Thorshavn and anchored, while the
Ben Machree went alongside; the little town was very picturesque,
a neatly-arranged collection of dolls' houses—or so they
appeared from a distance—each one of them a different colour.
They were most attractive, and no doubt many of the dolls
inside them were equally so. An hour after the *Ben Machree*
was due to sail, she was still alongside the pier; it seemed as
though the whole population was assembled there also.

"Ask her what's going on," I told the signalman, "I want
to be clear of this harbour before dark."

In due course the reply came back.

"Regret - delay. One - of - soldiers - due - for - leave - married - local - girl - this - afternoon. Shall - be - lucky - if - we -
sail - with - the - bridal - pair - only. Half - her - family - want -
to - come - as - well."

I hope that the marriage turned out happily; any bride that
starts her married life with two days at sea in a foreign trooper,
in war time and in a gale as well, deserves every success. While
we were still waiting for the *Ben Machree*, the British Naval

Officer-in-Charge and two of his staff came aboard *Ulster* to see us. It was blowing pretty strongly for August, and I remarked on the fact to one of our guests.

"My dear fellow," was his reply, "this is nothing. You should come up here in winter time. You see those streams flowing down the hillside over there? Well, in winter it blows so hard that the water goes up the hill backwards."

I refilled his glass. I thought that that yarn deserved it.

On return to Scapa, the Chief and I felt the desire for some exercise; we had not been ashore for ages. So we procured a couple of bikes from somewhere, and set off for a good spin into the wilds of Longhope. On return we were on the jetty at Lynesse awaiting our boat when two Wrens walked past. I recognised one as Nonsense-Constance the Wren driver I had met in Sunderland.

"Whatever are you doing up here?" I asked.

"I am a driver for the Naval Officer-in-Charge, Kirkwall," she replied.

We invited the two young ladies aboard *Ulster* two or three days later—strictly against orders, if I remember rightly. Anyhow they came, and a party of us went ashore to one of the islands for a picnic. Considerable organisation had been necessary to ensure their safe return to Kirkwall, and the skipper of the Lynesse-to-Kirkwall ferry had been persuaded— I know not how—to be ready to stop his ship in mid-Flow to embark these two girls from our motorboat at a certain hour.

After the picnic, therefore, our high-speed skimmer roared across the Flow to the appointed rendezvous. It was one of those perfect warm, still evenings that come so seldom to Scapa, and the noise of our boat's engine carried far and wide. As if this was not enough to make us conspicuous, just as we went past the battleship *Duke of York*, Flagship of Admiral Sir Bruce Fraser, my friend Constance took it into her head to stand up in the sternsheets of the boat, her blonde curls streaming in the breeze and glowing in the last rays of sunset. I felt that every eye in the *Duke of York*, including that of the Admiral, was focussed on our boat at that instant, and fully expected a signal ordering me to repair on board next day with an explanation, but nothing happened.

Oddly enough, not long afterwards I did find myself

before the Admiral, but in rather more formal circumstances. This was in connection with the visit of King George VI to the Fleet that month. He came across from Thurso in the destroyer *Onslow*, escorted by *Ulster* and another destroyer. We did this short trip at thirty knots, and then went alongside the destroyer depot ship *Tyne*; the crews of the three destroyers then mustered on board *Tyne* for inspection. By a stroke of luck, one of the press photographers present snapped the King as he was walking down the ranks of *Ulster's* crew.

When the Admiral presented me to the King, the latter said "Good afternoon, Donald," and then added, as he spotted my D.S.C. ribbon, "I see we have met before. Where did you get that?"

Not expecting the question, and also being a trifle nervous, I replied, "In the *Black Swan*, sir."

The King exchanged grins with the Admiral.

"Sounds rather like a pub to me," he said.

The next day the Fleet put to sea, with the King aboard the *Duke of York*, for gunnery practice and dummy air attacks; *Ulster* was one of the destroyer screen for the heavy ships. It was a very exhilarating and comforting sight to see the huge salvoes from the battleships straddling the target; the bright sunshine and strong breeze added to the magnificence of the scene, and all went well.

Back in harbour that night, after the order had been given for the Fleet to splice the mainbrace, there was a certain amount of minor celebration among the destroyers down in Gutter Sound. We collected some nurses from the *Isle of Jersey*, and went to call on my old friend and term mate, John Hodges, C.O. of one of the "O" class destroyers at the next buoy. We found him entertaining his brother-in-law, Captain Anthony Kimmins, who had slipped away from the King's party for a few minutes. We had a remarkably enjoyable evening, and I heard afterwards that next day the King commented in jocular fashion on Kimmins' rather wan features.

After another visit to the Faroes, from whence we carried out two anti-submarine sweeps in filthy weather and without result, *Ulster* returned to Rosyth for a boiler-clean and four days' welcome leave. We then had orders to sail to Plymouth in September.

The trip was northabout, and I took special care to see that we passed through the Minches in daylight. The trip was uneventful, but we all got a nasty shock on arrival at Plymouth; after the terrible bombing suffered by the city, it was almost unrecognisable. However, there was not much time to worry about past horrors, for within a very few hours after our arrival I found myself at a high-level conference to discuss the latest of the enemy's brainwaves in that connection—the glider-bomb.

This bomb was virtually the forerunner of all present-day guided missiles: it was launched from a bomber in the usual way, but then its downward path was controlled by wireless from the aircraft, and it could be guided towards the target with great accuracy. It was, therefore, a far more deadly affair than the normal bomb.

Just previously in the Bay of Biscay, the sloop *Egret* had been hit and sunk by one of these missiles in broad daylight; by a stroke of luck, however, an officer on deck in another ship close by had the quick-wittedness to take some photos of the incident. One of them showed the bomb passing close over-head, and this—plus other evidence—clearly proved that the horror was controlled from an aircraft, and guided onto the target.

At this time, the Navy and Coastal Command were starting operations on a large scale against the U-boats in the Atlantic and Bay of Biscay. This offensive was largely inspired by the late Captain F. J. Walker, one of the most famous Naval leaders in the war.

Walker was a remarkable man. Passed over for promotion to Commander in peace time, he soon proved his worth in time of war. He was a man of medium height, rather stocky build, dark complexion and firm steady eyes. His whole manner was one of quiet confidence and intense determination.

Whilst he agreed that escorts should defend a convoy, he was obsessed with the idea of attacking the U-boats before they could get within vulnerable distance of the convoys. For the first few years of the war there were not enough warships to spare to form these attacking groups, but when the shipyards were turning out new ships in large numbers Walker's plan became feasible. This was roughly it.

Small groups of sloops or destroyers patrolled certain areas of the sea, particularly the Bay of Biscay, in co-operation with aircraft of Coastal Command. If a U-boat was spotted by one of the latter, the group was directed by wireless to the area, and the hunt began; in addition, of course, the groups often detected and killed a U-boat by their own Asdic efforts. These offensive operations—as opposed to the purely defensive escorting of convoys—were just promising to be most successful.

At the meeting referred to, which was attended by a party of Admiralty officials and officers from the Admiralty, the photographs of the glider bomb were passed round, and the news of this latest enemy weapon was the cause of a certain amount of alarm and despondency. It was even suggested that these offensive patrols should be called off for the time being. Captain Walker himself was at the meeting, and I could see that he was getting more and more fed up at this suggestion. At last he could stand it no longer. I do not remember his exact words, but they were roughly as follows—

"Cancel the patrols? On the contrary, I propose that we move them closer inshore, deliberately within range of this aircraft, to tempt them to try again. The more they do, the more we shall find out about these new things, and the sooner the better. Moreover, I propose that some of the Admiralty officers should come out with the ships on patrol, and see with their own eyes."

His words were like a breath of fresh air in a stuffy room, though they were not received with great enthusiasm by some of those present. Almost at once, *Ulster* was ordered out to sea with another destroyer *Grenville*, the leader of the "U" Class Flotilla, to rendezvous with the sloop *Crane*, then at sea, and do a ten-day patrol in the Bay of Biscay. The main object was to try and catch a U-boat or two either as they went out on patrol, or returned to the French bases they were then using— Brest and L'Orient. The second objective I kept to myself— or so I thought.

"Operation 'Guinea-Pig', I understand, sir?" said Number One as we left harbour.

At daylight the first morning out we had the first thrill, appropriately enough not far from the Wolf Lighthouse; it was a misty day with a low cloud ceiling, and out of the latter there suddenly swooped a four-engined enemy Focke-Wulf. For a horrid space it hovered right overhead, then disappeared to the eastward.

"One of them there —— Wolves," I heard the signalman confide to his mate.

The minor excitements continued during the night; on several occasions, aircraft zoomed low over our heads in the dark. They were almost certainly our own, since we had been informed of these searches by Coastal Command, but it was an unpleasant form of entertainment. By night, a destroyer on the surface is very similar to a U-boat in the eyes of an over-keen bomb-aimer; luckily for us, nobody ever pressed the button.

On three separate occasions we sighted ships at night which were fully lighted up; these turned out to be our own hospital ships, whose movements were reported to us by signal from base every day. But, as Senior Officer of the Force, I invariably ordered *Grenville* and *Crane* to close with me and investigate from a discreet range; for at that time enemy blockade runners, with valuable cargoes from the Far East, were trying to slip into Brest and L'Orient. Knowing the enemy as we did by then, we were certain he would try any sort of subterfuge to achieve his end; for a blockade-runner to be disguised as a hospital ship, and to burn full navigation lights at night was just the sort of thing to expect. However, all our three suspects proved to be friendly, though doubtless their respective officers on watch had a nasty shock if they sighted us bearing down on them at high speed in the darkness.

We ourselves had a minor alert by daylight, when an unknown radar contact was picked up some twelve miles to the northward; its size clearly indicated a surface ship, and I hastily thumbed through the latest situation report.

"No friendly ship for miles around," I told Number One. He pressed the Alarm Bell and we went to Action Stations. I signalled the other two ships to close *Ulster*, and ordered full speed ahead on a north-easterly course to get between the enemy (if it was such) and his base. It was a dull grey morning, with a calm sea, visibility about five miles; we hurtled along in a most exhilarating manner.

"Bearing three five eight degrees, twenty thousand yards!"

The range closed rapidly, and we gained bearing to the eastward of the target in a most satisfactory fashion.

"Three five seven degrees, eighteen thousand!"

As the reports came up to the bridge, I could sense the tremor of excitement in the usual sing-song tones of the operator.

"Three five six degrees, sixteen thousand!"

If it were a blockade runner, or even a surface raider, I felt sure we could put up a pretty good show between us; the plan was to try and attack the enemy from three different points of the compass, *Ulster* and *Grenville* firing torpedoes so that they reached the target simultaneously. It was unfortunate that *Crane* had no torpedoes, and her maximum speed was about ten knots less than *Ulster* and *Grenville*.

"Three five five degrees, fourteen thousand!"

The forward guns were trained on the bearing; on the bridge every eye was glued to the horizon; we should sight her any moment now. I called to Birtwistle in the director.

"Stand by!"

As I spoke the signalman's excited voice drowned mine.

"Ship bearing red five, sir!"

For a few seconds there was dead silence on the bridge. Then I lowered my glasses in disgust; the enemy turned out to be a piddling little coaster, flying the flag of the Irish Free State, and proceeding southwards on its harmless, uninteresting course. We confirmed its identity, and swept past cursing; it was all I could do not to order "Open Fire!", and blow it out of the water.

"All right, relax everybody."

We resumed our patrol, and the same night our hopes were raised once more by the radar operator.

"Small echo range six thousand yards, bearing two hundred."

We altered course towards it, and once again my pulse quickened.

"Bearing two hundred, range five thousand!

This looked very like a U-boat on the surface, which was where it would be at night, either on passage or charging batteries.

"Bearing one nine eight, range three thousand!"

I waited a few minutes longer; the short-range weapons were trained on the target, and "B" gun loaded with starshell.

"Open fire starshell!"

At the speed we were steaming, this would be enough to illuminate the target, get a few rounds off before the U-boat (if it was one) dived, and give us a first-class bearing for the Asdic set to pick up the target under water. But "B" gun failed to open fire. Some ass had hung a scarf or other similar rag on the breech, thus jamming the firing mechanism. Meanwhile the radar contact disappeared from the screen, which was to be expected if it was a U-boat and had dived on sighting us. We closed in on the last bearing, and swept around with our Asdic, but failed to pick up a contact.

I was very angry to hear the reason that prevented "B" gun firing; on such small items did the difference between success and failure hang. I subsequently had the Captain of the gun's crew up before me as a defaulter, since it was his responsibility to see that that sort of thing did not happen, and stopped his gunnery specialist pay for some weeks.

Our patrol continued without scoring any successes, and with only one further incident. Once again it was a radar report—at dawn this time—and even more tantalising. For on closing the contact full of hope, we sighted nothing but a small decoy buoy; these were slipped by U-boats with that very purpose of luring any hunting craft away from the main target. We had been sold a real pup once again.

"All this standing by for action, and then damn-all turning up," moaned one of the officers; "wonder when we'll ever have a bash at the bastards."

"Don't worry," I assured him, "it'll come soon, and when it does, it will come quicker than you think."

CHAPTER XI

NIGHT ACTION

ON OUR return to Plymouth, we found ourselves ordered to take part in several night sweeps along the French coast in search of enemy shipping. These sweeps involved the force concerned leaving Plymouth at sunset, dashing at speed across the Channel on a southerly course to within a mile or so of the French coast, and then patrolling up and down for about two hours, before returning in a similar manner to arrive at Plymouth at dawn.

The first two nights *Ulster* and *Grenville* went in company with the light-cruiser *Phoebe*; the three of us steamed along on a course which silhouetted us against the moon—which I thought rather rash—but nothing happened. Every now and then mysterious lights flashed from the darkness of the coast close on our beam; perhaps some Frenchmen had sighted us and thought we were the spearhead of the long-awaited invasion. These night prowls were quite exciting, and just as much of a strain when nothing happened as when at last it did.

On Sunday, 3rd October, *Ulster* received orders to sail that night with our old friend *Grenville*, and three "Hunt" Class destroyers, *Tanatside*, *Wensleydale*, and *Limbourne*, under the command of the last named. In the forenoon once again I had a strong premonition that at last we were going to get a spot of action, and I sent for Sub-Lieutenant Rutherford, the Confidential Books officer.

"I think we had better land as many of these blasted C.B.'s and Signal Books as possible before sailing."

"Yes, sir, there's dozens we never use."

He and I spent hours bagging them up, making the list out, and getting them carted off to the local C.B. office ashore. It was an awful sweat, but as it turned out, it was the wisest thing we did that day. Just before sailing, a Midshipman (E) called

Brown came on board, and asked if he could come out with us for the night's trip.

"Yes, certainly, though I don't suppose you'll see much."

An R.A.F. officer turned up aboard *Grenville* also.

We sailed about eight o'clock, just as darkness was falling. The trip across to the French coast was uneventful, and we arrived at our ordered position about eleven; here we altered to a south-westerly course in single line ahead at fifteen knots, in the order *Limbourne*, *Tanatside*, *Wensleydale*, *Ulster*, and *Grenville*. We were zigzagging independently in succession, and thus the line proceeded like a snake wriggling along over the grass. It was a dark night, with a westerly wind and a slight swell.

The crew were closed up at Surface Action Stations, and we settled down to the usual long night of waiting. On our port beam the French coast was a low, dark blur with an occasional light twinkling here and there.

Then it happened.

Just before midnight the R/T on the bridge started crackling: "Destroyers from *Limbourne*. Contact bearing one nine zero, four miles." This was on the port bow of our force between us and the coast, and certainly looked interesting. I sang out to the Gun Control Position.

"Alarm bearing Red Four Zero!"

Almost immediately another signal came from *Limbourne*.

"Four Zero Blue."

This was an order for all destroyers to turn immediately 40 degrees to port together, with the object of bringing us all approximately in line abreast, steering towards the contact. Unfortunately the second and third in the line, *Tanatside* and *Wensleydale*, made a mistake and followed the leader *Limbourne* round in line ahead. This was a pity as it reduced our fire power, and resulted in two of our side being left at a disadvantage as regards range when the battle started.

Almost at once I sighted the enemy—several dark shapes steering eastwards across our bows from starboard to port; I quickly moved my gunsight onto the bearing, thus automatically signalling the gun control to follow, and immediately the guns trained round after it onto the target. Then everything happened at once; reports and signals from all sides.

"Ships bearing Green two zero, sir!"

"Alarm Starboard!"

"Signal from *Limbourne*, sir—Engage Enemy Bearing One Nine Zero!"

"Forward guns on target, sir!"

"Signal from *Limbourne*, sir—Speed Twenty-five Knots."

It was an exciting moment. I gave the order "Open fire, starshell" and increased speed. As the first starshell went off from "B" gun, I ordered "Open Fire main armament!". I could hear the sound of gunfire from the other ships, and in a few seconds night was turned into day. Ahead of us were five enemy destroyers of the "R" Class, and some light craft; in the glare of the starshell they appeared dead white, exactly like the models in the gunnery school. In fact I muttered to myself "It's just like Whaley!" as I gazed at them spellbound for a few seconds.

But it was no time for dallying. As the *Ulster* leapt forward towards the enemy into action for the first time, I had a quick look round to imprint in my memory where everybody was. The great thing about a night action is to try and get a clear picture of where each ship is; it is not by any means easy even at the start, and it becomes harder as every minute passes.

To port and fairly close was *Grenville* steering a parallel course; to starboard but further off were *Limbourne*, *Tanatside* and *Wensleydale* in line ahead instead of in quarter line, due to the error aforementioned. All were for the moment clearly visible in the light of the enemy's starshell, now bursting over our heads and making us feel uncommonly naked.

The enemy ships—whose armament, four 4.1-inch guns apiece was almost identical with ours—were still steering across our bows from starboard to port, so we automatically altered course to port to get parallel to them and engage them with all our guns, firing to starboard. It was a magnificent moment—five destroyers on each side banging away at each other, and a few light craft dodging about in between. By this time we had almost completely reversed our original course, and thus *Grenville* led our line—albeit rather straggly now—with *Ulster* second and the other three astern.

After a few minutes the enemy began to draw ahead. I at once increased "Full Speed" to get ahead of them if possible so as we could fire torpedoes, and *Grenville* did the same. The three "Hunt" class destroyers had no torpedoes, and were only able to muster twenty-six knots (about five knots less than ours), and so began to drop astern. However, there we were at the beginning of the show all fully engaged. It was a fine sight.

This was the moment that for months we had been waiting and training for: I felt completely at ease, and thoroughly exhilarated as round after round went off with comforting regularity. I wanted to shout at Birtwistle "Go on, hit the bastards!", but I restrained myself; I knew all his attention would be riveted on watching the fall of shot; to have interrupted would have been fatal, and besides I myself had a dozen other things to think about.

"Steer zero eight eight, Coxswain."

"Aye, aye, sir."

Just then one of the enemy light craft appeared close on our beam; I distinctly saw its silhouette and mentally registered it as an "R" boat. Our Bofors opened fire, started hitting at once, and it disappeared in a cloud of flame and smoke. I was sure we had sunk it. I turned again to the leading enemy destroyer, now only about two miles away—we were gaining on them. A few more minutes and we would be in a position to fire torpedoes; if *Grenville* and ourselves could get sixteen of them into the water about the same time, we stood a good chance of success. I called to Rutherford, who was Torpedo Control Officer.

"Get torpedoes ready starboard!"

"Aye, aye, sir!"

I heard him passing the orders to the tube crews by phone— I was wildly excited at the thought of scoring with a "fish".

SPLASH!

A great shower of water descended on the bridge, and soaked me and my binoculars. I wiped them angrily.

"What the hell——?"

Then I realised that the enemy had got our range only too well. I altered course five degrees towards him; all our guns were still firing flat out. After about ten minutes of this exhilarating performance, several things happened at once. The rear two of the enemy turned about on a reverse course and disappeared from our ken; the three "Hunts" went after them but at the time I could not be sure. Then just on our port bow, a tremendous flash occurred on *Grenville's* upper deck aft, and she stopped.

"*Grenville's* been hit, sir," said the signalman.

We swept past her. A quick glance showed a fire on one of her after-gun mountings, but there was nothing we could do about it, so we pressed on at full speed, still firing away. But the situation was not so funny now, as with *Grenville* stopped and the three "Hunts" fading away astern taken up with their own spot of action, we were the only one left to take on the three leading enemy ships. The range was now down to about three thousand yards, and splashes appeared all around us.

"We've hit her all right!"

Through my glasses I could see two red glows on the upper deck of the leading ship; it was an encouraging sight, and I thought excitedly, "If only we can sink her!" Suddenly there was a terrific bang and a flash on our own upper deck forward, and "A" gun ceased firing. I called my messenger.

"Find out what's up with 'A' gun."

Almost as I spoke *Ulster* gave a shudder. There was no sound, but the ship seemed to move sideways through the water; it was as though a giant had punched her amidships; I can remember the sensation distinctly even today. I realised at once that we had been hit again; however, the ship was still tearing along through the water, and the after guns firing away merrily. I called to Rutherford.

"Torpedoes ready yet?"

"Yes, sir."

At that moment all of us on the bridge were drenched with the splash of an enemy salvo falling just short, and "B" gun ceased firing starshell. We could not see the enemy too well, but I decided to have a bash with the torpedoes.

"Stand by to fire!"

I swung the ship to port to bring the sights on, and through the noise I could hear Rutherford calling "FIRE ONE! FIRE TWO! etc." Then I brought the ship's head back again to starboard, but it was obvious that all was not well.

"Captain, sir?"

"Yes?"

Someone was reporting to me.

"One shell hit just aft of 'A' gun, sir—most of the crew casualties. Another hit below the stokers' mess deck, sir. Forward magazine is flooded."

The starshell for "B" gun were supplied from the forward magazine—that meant no more illumination unless we used the searchlight. To do so would give the enemy an excellent aiming mark, but I reckoned he could see us pretty well anyhow, and it was essential to get our own guns on the target and firing flat out again. So I decided to close the range, and give the Bofors a real chance as well.

I altered in towards the enemy, now only about 2,000 yards off, and switched on the searchlight on the leading ship. It showed up white as paint, and the Bofors opened fire at once, with a comforting succession of steady thuds. I could see the bullets hitting the target, then I switched the searchlight off. "A" gun opened fire again much to my satisfaction.

I do not know what sort of shells the enemy was using, but I could see their main armament coming at us only too clearly. They lobbed over quite slowly, and every one looked as though it was going to land plumb on my head; it surprised me at the time what a height they were rising to, and the thought flashed through my mind "Just like a niblick shot". Fortunately by altering close in as I had done, I had put the enemy off range for a vital few minutes, and all his niblick shots went well over.

"Captain, sir?"

The Sub was calling from the charthouse.

"Yes?"

"The plot shows that we are heading for some shoals, we ought to alter course out to seaward."

In the excitement of the battle I had not given a thought to navigation; it would be disastrous to risk grounding with a damaged ship close off an enemy-held coast. Just before I put the wheel over, Rutherford reported that not all the torpedoes had been fired; I had swung the ship too quickly the first time.

"O.K. Fire them as the sights come on."

It was a thousand to one chance, but there was no point in wasting it. As we fired, the enemy turned away behind smoke, and the last sight of them I had was of a fire burning fiercely in the leader. I glanced at my watch. It was ten to one; the party had lasted fifty minutes, though it seemed much less.

"Captain, sir."

It was the Chief speaking.

"I'm afraid things are not too good down below, sir. The stokers' mess deck, both forward magazines and the forward low power room are flooded, sir. That second shell hit us on the water line just at a bad spot. We've stopped the flooding, but it's a question of the electric power; repair parties are on the job now, sir."

"Good—well, do your best, Chief. The party's over now anyway. We're heading back for Plymouth."

"Aye, aye, sir."

Number One stepped up onto the platform beside me.

"The wounded are in the wardroom, sir. The Doc's doing his best, but some of them are pretty bad, especially the Chief Cook and one of the ordinary seamen from 'A' gun's crew."

"I'll come down and see them in a minute."

"Very good, sir."

"We knocked hell out of that first ship anyway. I wish we'd got a fish into her, though. Hey what the hell's happening?"

As I was speaking, *Ulster* began to list to starboard in a most alarming way. (Oh God, I thought, I'm going to lose her after it's all over.)

"I'll nip down and find out, sir."

Number One left the bridge quickly; after a few minutes the ship resumed her even keel, and we sped on back across the Channel. I gave a call down the voice-pipe to the wireless office.

"How's life down there?"

Petty Officer Telegraphist Gasnier's voice was quite calm and cheerful.

"Transmission's gone for the moment, sir, though we can receive O.K. I'll let you know when we can send a message out, we're doing our best. The other ships are calling us, but at the moment we can't answer."

I could imagine that that would cause a certain amount of alarm, but there was nothing we could do about it except steer for home and hope for the best. Fortunately the engines were not affected, and we did a full-power run across the Channel in wet, misty weather.

In due course things straightened themselves out: we relaxed from Action Stations, the damage control parties contrived some order out of the chaos, and power for transmitting was restored. We sent a signal to Plymouth and *Limbourne*, and just before daylight we fetched up by the Eddystone. I went below and had a few words with the wounded in the wardroom; it was a sad sight, as some were clearly in a very bad way, but the Doc was attending to them quickly and confidently.

Chief Petty Officer Cook had been badly knocked about by the first shell that struck just after of "A" gun, where he was standing as one of the ammunition supply; pale and heavily bandaged, he lay on a stretcher hardly breathing; yet when I spoke to him he smiled back bravely, and I felt at the same time both proud and humble to have been in action with men like him. After a night that seemed endless, we made a rendez-vous with *Limbourne* and *Grenville* and steamed into the Sound. Just as we passed the breakwater in the grey light of dawn, it was reported to me that one of our wounded had died—the ordinary seaman from "A" gun's crew. I was very upset at the news, but concealed my feelings as best I could.

As we glided up harbour, we passed a ferry full of people who pointed at us excitedly, as well they might. We had two large shell holes forward, one on the waterline and one on the bulkhead by "A" gun, as well as many other obvious signs of battle here and there.

"Ring off main engines."

I gave the order at last with considerable feelings of relief, and went down to my cabin, where a scared but purring Georgie was peeping out from under my bunk. I flopped on a chair, so tired I could hardly think. After some sort of a wash and breakfast, we spent the forenoon trying to piece together the various phases of the action, but it was not easy. The other ships of our force had returned safely, with minor casualties and damage, though *Grenville* also had one man killed, and suffered almost similar flooding to ours.

On examination, we found that we had shipped over four hundred tons of water forward in the two magazines, stokers' mess decks, and the officers' cabin flat. The shell had pierced the side at the very worst possible place from our point of view —at the junction of two vertical bulkheads and two horizontal decks. All personal possessions in the stokers' mess and officers' cabin flat were, of course, completely flooded out. Repairs to the damage were estimated at three weeks, and in view of that, one watch was sent on leave on the same day that we entered harbour. I stayed on board for the first half of the repair period, and tried to write a coherent account of the night's proceedings. During that time, aerial reconnaissance over the French coast showed two German destroyers badly damaged in the small harbour of Lannion into which they had retired after the action. They remained there for six months, whereas our repairs were effected in four weeks.

So I suppose we could count it a draw in our favour, though I would have liked to have blown one of the enemy sky high. Still, we had done our best, and at the end of my report of proceedings I wrote—"H.M.S. *Ulster* has been in commission for three and a half months. This was her first-ever ship's action, and for many of the younger men aboard, their first time in action. This exciting encounter has had a very good psychological effect on all concerned, and I am happy to report that the bearing of all officers and men was very satisfactory."

At home on leave shortly afterwards, I was telling some friends about this adventure. When I had finished—

"And where were you while all this was going on?" asked an elderly lady, "were you asleep in your bed all the time?"

PART FOUR

THE MEDITERRANEAN

Chapter XII

ALEXANDRIA, THE AZORES, ADRIATIC AND ANZIO

AT THE beginning of November, *Ulster* was ready for sea again. Many and varied were the buzzes on board as to our future movements; betting was about evens as to whether it would be the frozen north or the sunny Med. I sincerely hoped that it would be the latter, as three winters at sea in northern waters had been enough for me.

On the 12th November the battlecruiser *Renown* slid as unobtrusively as a battlecruiser can do into Plymouth Sound, and anchored in the most seaward position. Along with two other destroyer C.O.'s, Acworth of *Rocket* and Talbot of *Tumult*, I was ordered aboard, and we were ushered into the Captain's cabin. Captain W. E. Parry then gave us the dope.

It was to be a high-speed trip to Alexandria, and on board *Renown* would be the Prime Minister and his staff on their way to the Cairo Conference. The P.M. and his retinue, which included several Wren officers, arrived at Plymouth and embarked under the cover of darkness just before sailing time. It was blowing a full westerly gale as we slipped from our buoys at dusk, and joined *Renown* just outside the breakwater. Twenty knots was ordered before we reached Eddystone, and then speed was increased to twenty-seven as we turned our noses into the open Atlantic. It was no fun at all for the destroyers; we were taking it green all the time as we slammed our way into the huge rollers, and my sea cabin was flooded, thanks to some ass who left a voice-pipe cock open.

"What's the hurry, sir?" gasped Number One, wringing out his scarf, but I merely smiled an enigmatic sphinxlike smile. However the secret was soon out, for on the second afternoon, when the weather had improved somewhat, members of the P.M.'s staff and the graceful forms of the Wren officers were seen perambulating in the sunshine on *Renown's* quarterdeck.

After forty-eight hours we arrived at Gib as darkness fell over the Rock in more ways than one, for a stream of contradictory orders was received as to our movements, and to those of *Renown* also. Our immediate need was oil, and after entering harbour in the dark and securing to one oiler, we had only just started oiling when we were told to cast off and find another one, which was at anchor in the Bay. After some difficulty we discovered the tanker in question, with a number of merchant ships apparently at anchor all around it. It was not until later that we learnt they were all aground, put out of action by limpet mines stuck on their hulls after Italian one-man submarine attacks!

We completed oiling by three a.m., by which time *Renown* had continued on her way with additional escort from local destroyers. It was a brilliant moonlight night, and our next stop was Algiers. Just before steaming out of the Bay, a small motorboat came dashing up and secured alongside.

"Hold on, *Ulster*, I have some special stores for you."

An Army officer jumped inboard, and asked for me.

"What is it—confidential books?"

"No, sir—you'll laugh when you hear. Forty dozen botts of sherry for Winnie!"

We embarked the precious load and set off at high speed after the others; but the next morning we gained a possible U-boat contact, and so we never put in to Algiers at all. In fact, we never saw the *Renown* again until we were ordered into Malta at dusk forty-eight hours later. The blackout had been lifted in Malta then as it was no longer considered necessary, and, although it was a welcome sight, the bright lights did not make it any easier for us to find our way into harbour. Just as we nosed our way towards the boom inside the main breakwater *Renown*, from her buoys inside, shone a searchlight full on us. Doubtless the gesture was well meant, but for a moment or so we were completely blinded.

The next thing I knew was that we had run into the western half of the boom, though luckily at very slow speed. We disentangled ourselves, and eventually made our way alongside the oiler close by the Naval Hospital. While we were oiling most of the P.M.'s party had transferred to the cruiser *London*: three hours later we were at sea again, escorting her at high speed to Alexandria. We steamed in there at noon forty-eight hours later, having completed the trip from Plymouth—over 4,000 miles—in six and a half days. Not bad steaming at all! The precious sherry was taken over by me personally to the *London* in our motorboat, but to my great disappointment, I did not see the Prime Minister. He had been quite ill on arrival in Malta, and remained there for two days, finally arriving at Alexandria in *Renown* on 21st.

"Never mind, you'll probably get an O.B.E. for this in the New Year's Honours," remarked Commodore Dick with a grin; I am still waiting. However, I did get a pleasant surprise not long after that when *Ulster* met up with *Grenville*, and I went over to see Roger Hill, her C.O.

"Congratulations," he said, as I went into his cabin.

"What for?"

"The other half of your D.S.C. for the Channel Battle."

"—but I never did a bloody thing——"

"Captain (D) doesn't think that, any way. Seen his report on it?"

"No, I haven't."

Hill chucked it across. I read it quickly, and handed it back.

"All I can say is he must be thinking of two other chaps."

I was glad, however, that two or three other awards came to the *Ulster* after that little party. One of them was to the Leading Seaman in charge of "A" gun's crew—the man whom I had punished for his carelessness a few weeks' before. Of him I had written in my report:

"A shell bursting near 'A' gun killed one member of the crew, and wounded most of the others. This Leading Seaman, though himself wounded, rallied his gun's crew, reorganised the ammunition supply, and 'A' gun continued firing until the action was over."

He received a D.S.M., as did also the Petty Officer in charge of the Bofors gun. The Chief, Lieutenant Williamson, was mentioned in despatches for his efforts in connection with the damage control, but one or two others whom I had hoped might feature in the list were unlucky.

Ulster continued to be based at Gibraltar for some weeks for escort duties both eastward and westward. After one of the latter trips, we were ordered with *Rocket* and *Grenville* into Horta in the Azores to refuel. A rather unnerving spell followed, poking about in low visibility trying to find Horta, but we eventually arrived. As we berthed alongside the inevitable oiler that the Admiralty seems to provide in every corner of the globe, some ancient "Town" Class destroyers came in also; on board the *Chelsea*, leaning over the guardrail in a pair of even more ancient bedroom slippers, was a cousin of mine from home, Tom Pritchard by name. He was the M.O. on board; we had often met on leave out shooting and fishing, but we never expected to meet in such an out-of-the-way hole as Horta. It certainly was just about the dirtiest, most depressing spot I have ever seen in all my life. The weather was appalling, there were no attractions, except those we were warned against in the most horrific language, and hence shore leave was practically nil.

Ulster, *Grenville*, and *Rocket* were still sitting quietly there two or three nights later, when the nightly situation report signal was decoded and shown to me. The three of us were down in the signal as being about two hundred miles away in mid-Atlantic, escorting a convoy to the Mediterranean. I leapt out of my chair, ordered the other two ships to come to immediate notice for steam, and shortly afterwards the three ships were hurtling eastwards at high speed to try and pick up the convoy.

We found it at last and, in due course, were ordered to take the *Orontes* and another transport under our wing as "special ships" bound for Algiers; they were detached as the convoy passed Gib en route for the Cape. It was not a very happy trip, and I remember it in particular as an example of how a combination of minor annoyances can snowball into disturbing proportions.

We had not been able to get any fresh potatoes at Horta other than a somewhat sweet brand of yam, and the ship's company were considerably upset by this. We had hoped to put into Gib, where there was every chance that our Christmas mail would be awaiting us, but whilst still at sea we were ordered to proceed direct to Algiers; on receipt of that order I had included in my acknowledgment a request that mail for all three destroyers might be sent out by boat into the Bay, so that one of the destroyers could be detached and collect it— a matter of perhaps quarter of an hour's absence from the convoy—but this was not approved; and on entering the Med, instead of calm seas and warm sunshine, we were met with a nasty lop and a bitter east wind.

On Christmas morning, therefore, when we were about six hours' steaming from Algiers, I felt it was up to me to say a few words over the internal broadcasting system to the ship's company to try and boost morale, which I could sense was at a low ebb. I told Number One that I would do so, and took particular care over what I was going to say.

The trouble was that I never said it. For during the forenoon, a Possible U-boat was reported by aircraft right in the track of the convoy plumb ahead of us; and so, just before noon, when Number One reported that all was ready for me to speak to the ship's company (for which I had to leave the bridge to broadcast from my sea cabin), I told him to cancel it. The thought occurred to me that we would all look pretty silly—especially myself—if we were torpedoed when I was speaking. Admittedly it was a thousand-to-one chance, but thousand-to-one chances had a habit of coming off during wartime.

So I told him to cancel my short talk, nor could I tell him the reason why, since it would hardly make the men down below decks feel any more at ease to know that there was a U-boat lurking about. It was a wrong decision on my part, I know, and a very stupid one into the bargain, but that is what happened. I told him I would try and speak to the men when we got into harbour. But we had to oil first, and by the time that was completed and we had proceeded round to our berth in the main harbour and secured alongside, it was about seven p.m., and there was only an hour or so left for leave; in any case, none of the ship's company had any of the local currency. In the meantime, a succession of reasons had prevented me speaking to the ship's company as I intended; the main one being that a local staff officer came on board to discuss future movements for *Ulster*, and stayed for ages.

As far as the officers were concerned, when after dinner we all trooped over to call on the *Grenville* who was lying alongside, we found they had a party of Wren officers aboard, and it became very clear that no other visitors were particularly welcome.

On board *Ulster* I could sense that all the ship's company were as fed up as blazes, for the buzz had gone round that we were to sail the next day, and I turned in feeling angry and depressed myself. The latter mood was accentuated the next morning during censorship of the outward mail—one of the most hateful jobs of the whole war in my opinion; one young stoker had written home most bitterly, finishing with the words that ". . . even the Captain had let us down by not saying a few words to us today . . ."

That was the last straw, because I knew in my heart of hearts that he was quite right. I rang for the First Lieutenant.

"Clear Lower Deck at the earliest convenient opportunity."

"Very good, sir."

Well, I spoke to the ship's company. I could not say what I had intended to say the day before, but I explained why not; it was not a very good effort but I did my best. I finished by saying leave would be granted from the middle of the forenoon till half-an-hour before the time of sailing, which was four p.m.

I went back to my cabin and flung myself down angrily in my armchair. The morale of the ship's company was so vitally important, and I knew what a sensitive barometer it was: an elementary error of judgment on my part the day before had sent it plunging to rock bottom, and the resultant wave of gloom was now destined to spread to a hundred families at home.

Suddenly there was a knock on the door.

"Come in."

It was the young stoker whose letter had given me such a well-deserved kick in the pants. Whether he realised that fact I could not for the moment make out, but it did not matter in comparison with what he said. The words tumbled out over themselves.

"Excuse me coming to see you like this, sir, but it's about a letter I've written home. I've got things all wrong, sir—I wondered if—I could have it back again, sir. I want to tear it up and write another—there's just time before the mail goes, sir."

"Yes, of course you can get it back if you can find it. Ask the First Lieutenant, he's probably got the mail. Tell him I said so."

"Thank you very much, sir."

He darted to the door, but I called him back.

"Another thing," I said, "when you write home, try and keep your letters cheerful. Moans and groans won't help much the other end, you know."

"I realise that now, I'm very sorry, sir."

"That's all right," I replied, "I made a mistake, too, yesterday. Now we're both wiser, aren't we?"

He grinned, and disappeared quickly, but with a light-hearted step, and my own spirits rose accordingly.

We sailed that same evening with a convoy for Malta; this was uneventful, except for the welcome news whilst on passage that the *Scharnhorst* had been sunk in northern waters by the combined efforts of a mixed British force, including the *Duke of York*: the last time we had seen her guns firing was at Scapa when H.M. the King was aboard.

From Malta we went whizzing up the Adriatic to Brindisi to join Captain (D) 24, who was operating a mixed flotilla in that area for various little jobs. We moved on next day to Bari, which was a terrible harbour from which to work, being absolutely littered with wrecks: these were the result of a very successful surprise air attack some weeks previously.

One of the items on our programme was bombarding the coastal railway behind the enemy lines, even as far north as Ancona; it was quite an exciting business, since it had to take place in the dark, and we were never quite sure where the enemy minefields were. Moreover, there was always the risk of going aground in an over-enthusiastic desire to get as close to the railway as possible. Indeed, even Captain (D) himself had just previously taken *Troubridge* ashore, closely followed by *Tumult*, for what must have been an embarrassing few minutes; this was one case when one did not want to follow a senior officer's example.

The general plan was to wait, with guns loaded and trained on the railway, until a succession of flashes denoted the approach of a train on the electrified line, then to open fire and plaster the line ahead of it. Whether we ever did a great deal of damage was not easy to say, but we must have done a certain amount in addition to the effect on enemy morale. At any rate there was the comforting feature that the trains never fired back.

Another operation which was less popular was a patrol off the Jugoslav coast; once again there was the problem of navigation along an unlighted hostile coast at night, with no knowledge of the position of any minefields, or what we were likely to meet, except that anything we did would be unfriendly.

These patrols were a considerable strain, finishing up as they did with the dash back across the Adriatic, through the gap in our own minefield, keeping one's fingers crossed until we found it, then up harbour weaving past all the wrecks to the oiler; this as usual was tucked away in the most inaccessible corner of the harbour and, after a few hours' oiling, it entailed another spell fobbing about back to one's berth at a buoy or alongside another destroyer. Those "Fleet" Class destroyers were over 120 yards long, and in bad weather it was quite tricky work fiddling about in a harbour crowded with wrecks.

The weather was at its worst as 1943 passed on its way into 1944; and on New Year's Eve, five of the destroyers were ordered to sea at short notice to search for an alleged U-boat in mid-Adriatic. It was blowing a northerly gale and snowing hard, as all night long we swept in line abreast five miles apart up the middle of the sea. *Ulster's* position in the line led us very close to some small unlighted islands near Pelagosa, just to give us an added thrill.

The search was completely negative, and as we returned to Bari the next morning, we received a signal—"From Naval Officer-in-Charge. Happy New Year." The destroyer astern of me flashed "Suggest we reply—WITH KNOBS ON TO THE B.F. WHO SENT US TO SEA LAST NIGHT!" However, the C.O. thought wiser of it later, and the signal was never sent. Probably just as well.

It can be pretty cold in the Adriatic in wintertime, and I for one was mighty glad when the *Ulster* was ordered back to Malta to boiler clean. By then (January, 1944) Malta was beginning to recover fairly well from her long ordeal. There were opportunities for football and hockey, and a certain amount of the Island's pre-war gaiety was returning. It was a very enjoyable spell, and we all felt much better for it.

But the time passed only too quickly and, in what seemed no time at all, I found myself driving the *Ulster* into Naples Bay past the beautiful Isle of Capri; this was in strong contrast to the desolation of Naples. Both by sabotage and Allied bombing, the latter city and its harbour had been extensively damaged; there seemed to be even more wrecks in Naples harbour than there were in Bari.

Within a few hours of arrival I was summoned to a very high-level secret conference to discuss operation "Shingle", the proposed landing at Anzio. It was a very daring project, and deserved much greater success than it eventually had; a large Allied Force of two divisions was to be landed behind the enemy lines to cut their communication with Rome, and the long sandy beaches by the pleasant little seaside resort of Anzio were earmarked for the job. Great preparations were made for the operation, and the staff made quite sure everyone concerned knew everything about it.

As each Commanding Officer went into the conference room, he was handed a packet about the size of a London Telephone Directory.

"What's this?" I asked. "*Cook's Guide to Italy*?"

"The port you're just going to visit, anyhow," was the somewhat icy reply.

I personally was staggered at the complexity of the orders, and the rigidity of the programme, even down to the most minute detail. However, it was not for me to argue, I had enough to do to try and master the duties assigned to *Ulster* alone, especially as I found myself Senior Officer of a group of three destroyers escorting quite a large section of the assorted collection of landing craft.

This section was already mustered at Castellamare in a remote corner of Naples Bay, where we joined them at dusk on January 20th. Even to the dumbest of the dumb, it must have been apparent that a landing was due to take place somewhere, and excitement ran high; it amazes me to this day that the secrecy of the objective was maintained, especially in view of the casual outlook of some of my opposite numbers.

Ulster had just anchored at Castellamare and I was down

in my cabin wrestling with the invasion orders, when a signal was brought to me. It was from one of the other destroyers asking permission to give shore leave that night in Castellamare. I refused permission, and the Commanding Officer in question came over to see me.

"Leave?" I said. "Are you quite crazy? If you let your chaps ashore tonight, it only needs one bloke to get a bit full of the local brew and start nattering about tomorrow, and within two minutes the buzz will have reached Rome, and every bloody Hun in Italy will be on the beach to meet us."

Next morning, under blue skies and in brilliant sunshine, *Ulster* led a long line of ships out of the Bay on a southerly course between Capri and Sorrento. No less than fifty-six L.S.T.'s were included in the operation. At dusk we turned to the westward, and later to the north-westward, passing close to the dark and unlit Ponza group of islands. It was a frosty, starry night which passed without incident; by midnight 36,000 men and over 3,000 vehicles had been landed, and by the afternoon of the 23rd two divisions and a great deal of equipment had followed them. Opposition was nil and the enemy was taken by surprise; the only casualty at sea was the fighter-direction ship *Ulster Monarch*, damaged by a mine.

After the initial landing, *Ulster* was one of the force of destroyers ordered to patrol to seaward of the beaches to defend the stream of supply ships that followed the main assault. We steamed round and round on a ten-mile beat, and for three days nothing much occurred; we had good air cover, and the whole thing appeared to be a "piece of cake". We were ordered to return to Naples to refuel, and arrived there to see an astonishing sight quite unconnected with the war—Vesuvius in eruption.

Unfortunately the wind was from the north, and the clouds of fine dust that went up descended only on the Allied lines, doing an enormous amount of damage. On one airfield near Naples a large number of aircraft were put out of action; the ships in harbour suffered from the powdery stuff penetrating auxiliary machinery, and everyone suffered an irritation of nose and throat through breathing the dusty air all day and night. At one time in the middle of the day no shipping could move in or out of harbour due to the low visibility; not only that, but the filthy stuff lay everywhere in heaps; it did not melt like snow, and there was no rain to wash it away.

It was just at this time that *Ulster* was ordered over to Capri on a forty-eight hours "wallow-in-luxury-and-admire-the-scenery" jaunt, as the Staff officer put it. Unfortunately, the whole place was inches deep in dust, and our "sight-seeing wallow" was not very enjoyable.

Chapter XIII

"COMBING THE MED"

WHEN WE returned to the Anzio beachhead, the scene had changed considerably; instead of pushing forward, our forces had dug-in. The Germans had reacted very quickly to the Allied landing, and their strong counter attack on February 16th nearly drove our troops into the sea. The perimeter was considerably reduced, and air attacks upon it and upon our shipping in harbour increased in tempo, especially at dusk. Just before that time, the warships on patrol were recalled to the beachhead to give maximum A.A. protection, and to protect the ships at anchor by making smoke. This latter was a double-edged weapon from the point of view of ships under way.

One night I shall never forget; amongst the warships present were *Delhi* and *Spartan*, both cruisers, the latter almost brand new; she had been working up at Scapa six months previously at the same time as *Ulster*. It was a clear, frosty sunset, and as the sun dipped into the sea like a glowing ball of fire, it seemed to be an omen of what was going to happen. A very fierce air-raid followed, low-level torpedo bombers synchronising their attacks with high-level stuff, and streams of tracer bullets were flying in every direction.

We were only a few cables away from *Spartan* when she was hit; it was a glider-bomb, and I watched it descend like a comet relentlessly guided onto its target by the parent aircraft. It hit the cruiser amidships, and at once a large fire broke out. However, we could not help; we were far too busy zigging about in the clouds of smoke, firing away whenever we could. From the Bofors mounting came a report that they had shot a low-level bomber down into the sea, but I never saw it. I was far too busy conning the *Ulster* past an American destroyer, hit and on fire, but with all her guns still firing away.

At last the attack was over, and we were ordered to return to our patrol to seaward. About an hour later, I had gone down to my sea cabin for a few minutes rest, when there was a knock on the door.

"Come in."

It was Petty Officer Telegraphist Gasnier. His face was grave, and without a word he handed me a signal. "To C.-in-C. from *Delhi*. *Spartan* sunk."

I could hardly believe it, yet the next morning it was only too true. There she lay, keel up in shallow water like a great stranded whale. It seemed astonishing that a single bomb amidships could have sunk her so quickly. I felt sick and angry at the enemy's success.

Something which made us all even madder one evening later was the loss of one of our hospital ships. Fully illuminated with the Red Cross clearly visible on both sides, she was bombed and sunk as she was on passage from Anzio to Naples. From our position on patrol some miles away, we saw it happen, but could do nothing about it.

And so through February and early March the battle went on; in daytime we were often ordered to do some bombarding of enemy positions inshore. We would proceed along the coast and then, in co-operation with Army spotting officers ashore, loose off as many rounds as quickly as possible before the enemy could retaliate. This they did with a long-range gun mounted on the railway, or with other long-range guns near the coast. The moral effect of a single shell plopping at random into the water was not particularly pleasant. The destroyer *Loyal* was hit one day in her engine room with most inconvenient results.

After a week or ten days on patrol, the destroyers were relieved in turn to refuel and have a spell off duty. Naples was having its share of air raids just then, and some of the shipping was accordingly dispersed round the smaller harbours round the Bay.

On one occasion *Ulster* was ordered into the tiny port of Torre d'Annunciata; we squeezed in between the break-waters in bright moonlight, and secured alongside a merchant ship; the latter was berthed at a quay—the mainland side of the harbour. The ship was unloading potatoes to feed our enemies of six months before; the little town was in a pretty good shambles, and the weather was appallingly cold. The outlook was, therefore, not particularly bright. However, the first evening the local Port Officer, an R.N.R. Lieutenant, came aboard with a spot of unexpected good news.

"By the way," he remarked, "there's an Army hospital not far off down the road in some God-forsaken spot or other. They're having a pretty grim time, and I wondered if you'd care to ask some of the nurses aboard one night. I can fix transport."

Well, there was only one answer to that question. Next evening, half a dozen very delightful nurses from Army Hospital 103 arrived on board about seven o'clock: in addition to the usual line in food and drink, hot baths were provided for the guests.

"My, that was wonderful," said one of the girls returning to the wardroom, pink-faced and beaming. "If you could see the squalor in which we're living ashore—a bombed-out school; and before the Huns left they poured cement down all the drains and waste-pipes."

The party seemed to go with a swing, and there seemed no reason at all why we should not repeat the performance the next day. Not all the girls were able to turn up again, but some did so; however, in the course of the evening, a signal arrived with orders for us to sail next morning for the Anzio beachhead, so the second party broke up fairly early—well, before midnight anyway.

Before turning in, I noticed with some apprehension that it had come on to blow a bit from the west, and that some more ships had sought shelter in the enclosed harbour where we were, behind the breakwater to the westward of our berth. They were therefore directly to windward of us in our berth alongside the merchant ship, which was still alongside the landward quay. Just ahead of us, similarly berthed, was another merchant ship, and the destroyer *Kempenfelt*—the latter having only just arrived that evening.

I had hardly closed my eyes when the officer of the day aroused me.

"Blowing hard now from the west, sir, and raining like blazes. What's more, it looks as though that big merchant ship away to windward has dragged a bit—she seems closer to us, sir."

Cursing like hell, I pulled on some clothes and ran up on the bridge; through the rain and gloom I could see the towering form of the merchant ship considerably closer, but there was nothing I could do about it. Some landing craft had crept in and anchored between us and the entrance, and for us to get under way and try to leave harbour would have been madness. There was only one thing to do—stay put and hope for the best.

However, I ordered steam for immediate notice; the duty watch mustered on deck, and huddled miserably under the lee bulkhead up forward. Conditions were really miserable; wind howling through the rigging, accompanied by driving rain and clouds of black smoke from the merchant ship a few cables to windward. After about an hour stamping my feet, and peering unhappily through the gloom, it looked as though the merchant ship's anchors had held, and that all was comparatively well. I had just left the bridge, when there was a shout down the voice pipe.

"Merchant ship's started to drag again, sir, but she's drifting over in *Kempenfelt's* direction."

I hopped back onto the bridge to see the great hulk of the ship in question moving remorselessly down on *Kempenfelt*; it was literally a question of minutes before she would be quite flattened out. Her lamp flashed quickly.

"Am coming astern on to you."

Just in time she slid clear of the menace to windward of her, but she came astern with a vengeance, berthing with a tremendous crash on our port side. The next few hours were some of the most miserable I can ever remember in the whole of my life.

It was now blowing a full gale from the west, and even in the enclosed harbour where we were, an appreciable swell got up, causing all the ships to roll about considerably, even though secured alongside. *Ulster* being the jam in the sandwich between *Kempenfelt* and the potato ship suffered really badly. For in her hurry to leave her berth just previously, *Kempenfelt* had parted all her wires, and now one was round her starboard propeller, rendering her immobile. She had also dragged a pair of catamarans along with her, and these were now engaged in merrily punching a pair of holes in our side amidships. There were no tugs available, so all we could do was sit there and wait for the storm to die down, being ourselves more and more scarred and damaged with each bump. It was an agonising and helpless position.

At last the weather eased; I went ashore and my R.N.R. friend drove me to Naples to explain the position up at the Naval H.Q. When I had told my story—

"Could you not have moved out of harbour earlier in the evening," asked the Staff officer, "before it really started to blow hard?"

'I didn't think it advisable to start moving about in that tiny harbour in the dark when it was full of ships, sir," I replied; "we were quite happy where we were alongside."

"Very happy indeed," murmured my R.N.R. friend. I could have murdered the fellow.

"Um yes—well, I suppose so," said the Staffie.

The upshot was that after some temporary repairs in a small dockyard near Naples, *Ulster* returned to Malta to be properly patched up.

"Tough luck indeed," said Captain Eaton, when I reported to him ashore. "I don't think it was your fault when other ships were barging about and bumping into you. Anyhow, you've had a fairly hectic time up at Anzio lately, a couple of weeks here won't do you any harm. The troops will get some football, and at last there's a fair amount of beer in the canteen. By the way, if your young officers want to see a feminine face for a change, there's a very nice crowd of nurses up at the Naval hospital. Ask them on board one evening, if you feel like having a party. . . ."

Oddly enough, the next day when we were playing hockey against the R.N. Hospital, two very attractive naval nurses turned up to watch their team being beaten. We invited them on board for tea as compensation.

"Captain Eaton's orders," I explained.

These same two sisters, Betty and Kitty Cotton, were extremely charming, and in due course became honorary members of the *Ulster* wardroom. It was only natural, therefore, when the Malta Club's "mi-careme" dance came along that we should escort them along; Michael Marwood, my late Number One from *Verdun*, turned up from somewhere and joined us to make it a very hilarious evening, which nearly ended in disaster. For returning homeward in the high speed "skimmer", with the Chief driving at his usual suicidal pace past all the wrecks and other snags that beset Malta harbour, we passed under a wire joining two obstacles.

At that precise moment some of us stood up in the stern-sheets, and the wire whizzed a few inches over our heads. Had we been just that much taller we would have been decapitated.

An even nastier shock awaited me next morning. My little jest to Betty and Kitty about Captain Eaton's orders boomeranged on me to no mean tune. For when the telephone rang just after breakfast—

"Captain Eaton here," said his voice, "got a small job for you, Donald. The Captain of the *Tyrian*'s gone sick, and I want you to take over command of her temporarily. She arrives from Alex tomorrow, and sails the next day for Naples. You'll have to take her up there, and just stay put until we can find another permanent C.O. for her. It'll only be a matter of a week of two; sorry about this, but you are the only chap we can think of to do the job."

"Very good, sir."

I replaced the receiver inwardly fuming. The last thing in the world I wanted to do was to leave *Ulster*, even for a week, apart from the fact that my stand easy had vanished by the board. However, orders were orders.

Tyrian was a very new destroyer. She had worked up in Alex after coming out from home, and as far as I knew had never been in action. Under the circumstances, I was not particularly anxious to take her up into the schemozzle of the Anzio beachhead. However, I packed a suitcase, gave Georgie, my black kitten, a farewell pat, and stepped over the *Ulster*'s gangway with a definitely sinking feeling in my tummy.

"All the best, sir," said Number One.

"See you soon, sir," added the Chief.

"Keep your fingers crossed," I said.

When I joined *Tyrian* an hour before she sailed, I found the First Lieutenant in bed with 'flu, the Chief Gunner's Mate, about the most important rating aboard in war time, had just

F

been carted off ashore to the hospital, one of the officers had had his wine bill stopped for overdoing it, and a confidential signal book was missing. Apart from all that, there was nothing to worry me at all.

Tyrian was almost identical to *Ulster* in build and layout, in fact she had a later type of surface radar which was most useful, so I had no qualms about manoeuvring her. After a cold, wet trip, which included meeting a convoy head on in the Straits of Messina, we fetched up at Naples. The next night there occurred one of the worst air raids that the port had had for some time, and this was followed by a gale a few days later. As we lay wallowing at anchor in Naples Bay, with our stern a few cables from a most unpleasant lee shore, I began to wonder what I had done to deserve all this!

The next night when we were duty destroyer with steam at immediate notice, I was in my cabin reading a novel when I was handed two signals, both from the C.-in-C. The first read "Stand by to sail at 2300 tonight. Further orders follow." The second was more inviting. It was—"Request pleasure of your company at dinner tonight. Car will meet you at jetty at 1930."

Either signal by itself would have been quite clear, but the combination was rather odd. I made the necessary replies and arrangements on board, put on a clean collar, and duly went ashore. The Flag Lieutenant met me, and we went rocking off by car through the darkness.

"General Alexander's down here for a few days, and he wants to go up to Anzio to see for himself how things are. You will meet him at dinner, and then take him up afterwards."

The Naval C.-in-C., Admiral Sir John Cunningham, was then living in a villa outside Naples, which had been owned by Lady Hamilton a hundred years or more before; for once I was literally following in Nelson's footsteps. For a junior officer like myself to sit down to dinner with both Naval and Military C.-in-C.'s at the same table was an affair not easily forgotten. After a very pleasant evening, the Admiral bade me good night.

"Take great care of the General," he said, "you are responsible for him entirely. Remain at Anzio as long as he wishes, and then bring him back here."

The trip up was without incident during the night, and as soon as we arrived off the beachhead, the General went ashore. At that time the perimeter held by the Allies was remarkably small, and the enemy was able to lob shells into the harbour, a very annoying pastime from our point of view. We kept a discreet distance away, in view of our special responsibility, until about three o'clock in the afternoon, when the General returned aboard.

"What now, sir?" I asked.

"If you could get me back to Naples by seven-thirty, I would be very glad," he replied smilingly.

The distance to go was 130 miles—a full power run would do it nicely.

"We'll do our best, sir," I replied.

We made it by five minutes; the only mishap en route was when a rather sharp alteration of course upset the General's cup of tea down in my cabin. He had a most charming manner, putting all of us at our ease, and talking cheerfully and inform-ally; we hoped to glean some information about the forth-coming Second Front, but there were no flies on the General in that respect!

A few days later another Lieutenant Commander turned up from somewhere to take over command of *Tyrian*—it turned out he had been at school with my brother—and I was left with the small personal problem of getting back to Malta and the *Ulster*. Everywhere I applied, the usual hydra of official obstructionists reared their heads. Eventually I discovered a transport plane left for Malta at dawn the next day, and I applied for a seat in it.

"Can't promise anything," said a harassed transport officer, "every plane here going anywhere is booked up completely for weeks ahead; but roll up to the airfield tomorrow morning on spec, if you like. Five-thirty on the dot."

Next day in the half-light of a perfect Mediterranean dawn I found myself looking down into the crater of Vesuvius from a Dakota. Except for the crew of four very cheerful South Africans, I was the only other member of the "completely booked up" aircraft. A couple of hours later I was at Malta, seated in my cabin aboard *Ulster* with a glass of beer in my hand, and Georgie purring a full-throttle welcome on my knee!

As usual, everything had turned out all right.

"Nice work, sir," said the Chief, "now we can have a party."

"Saint Patrick's Day, sir," added Number One, "can't let that go by without doing something."

We soon fixed up about twenty guests—"Glad you've forgiven me, Donald," grinned Captain Eaton. We rigged up the wardroom all Irish fashion, with shamrocks and so on *ad lib*; even Georgie had a green ribbon for the occasion. About nine o'clock—

"Stand by, sir," whispered Number One.

A minute or so later, I was handed a signal which puzzled me considerably.

"What's up?" asked Captain Dippy Evans, who was also a guest, "stand by for action?"

I handed him the signal, and he read it out aloud to all the others.

"To *Ulster* from Belfast. Greetings to all on this solemn occasion. Stand by to receive me at nine o'clock. Signed Saint Patrick."

The lights then went out except for a spotlight on the door. Muttered oaths and heavy breathing broke the silence, and then Number One and the Gunner staggered in bearing on a chair the outsize figure of our genial Irish Doc, William Johnston. The latter was robed in a sheet, the only visible part of him being his glistening red dial, surmounted with wig, whiskers and beard that must have comprised our complete stock of sick bay cotton wool. Beaming beer and bonhomie, the Saint delivered a stirring oration in his native brogue; then he ambled gravely round the wardroom, greeting each officer with a dignified bow, and each nurse with a kiss.

Trust the Doc not to miss a golden opportunity like that!

Repairs completed, *Ulster* returned to the Anzio beachhead, where air attacks and midget submarine activity were the order of the day. A division of destroyers was permanently on duty to seaward of the very open anchorage, where the shipping that arrived was only just enough to supply the Army. The enemy had reacted to operation "Shingle" in great strength, and although the Allies' position in March was not quite so precarious as it had been at one time, stalemate seemed to have set in.

Our patrols were very strenuous: we had to be on the alert the whole time, for attacks when they did come, came with amazing speed, generally from landward by low-flying aircraft, which were difficult to see against the land. It was one such attack that sank the destroyer *Janus*, and my old friend Shorty Morrison, her Captain, was not among the survivors.

The enemy was also then replying most pugnaciously to any destroyer detailed to steam close inshore for bombardment duties. I must confess that it was not pleasant when the return fire fell within a few yards of the ship's side; a destroyer was quite a decent-sized target for a land gunner to fire at. One afternoon, the first shell was very short, but gradually the splashes crept closer and closer; there was dead silence on our bridge in between our own salvos, and I could sense a feeling of strain.

As I have said before, any C.O. does not worry so much about his own particular skin, but about his ship and the lives of his ship's company. I certainly did not want the *Ulster* to be hit again, or to suffer any more casualties. Looking round the bridge personnel, I saw a very young rating, clearly in the grip of terror, staring over the side in the direction from which the shells were coming; his eyes were popping out of his head, and I thought any moment he might break down.

"Let's have a cup of tea, shall we?" I said loudly to nobody in particular, "Jones, pop down to my cabin and tell my steward, will you?"

His attention was diverted from the arrival of the next shell, which was very close, he pulled himself together, and all was well.

The destroyers on patrol were a mixed lot from the various flotillas out there; one of the Captains (D) at the time was Captain Beaky Armstrong in *Laforey*, a most dynamic character who hated being in harbour, and was all for offensive action against the enemy at every possible moment.

"Come on, chaps," he would say, "let's comb the Med. for these damn U-boats."

In the early hours of March 21st, *Laforey*, *Tumult* and *Ulster* were doing a spot of combing along the convoy route between

Messina and Naples. We were zigzagging along in line abreast about a mile apart on a north-easterly course, with *Ulster* in the right-wing position. The weather was perfect, and as no C.O. could stay on the bridge permanently, I had gone down to my sea cabin for a short snooze. At 0450 the bell beside my ear rang.

"Asdic operator reports contact bearing green two zero, range one thousand, possible submarine."

"O.K., I'll come up."

We had had many a false alarm, but I nipped up on the bridge, and put on the spare earphones. At once all trace of weariness vanished. Even to my unpractised ear it was definitely a submarine.

"Drop a depth-charge!"

That was the standard drill to put the U-boat off his aim; we then signalled the other two ships, and the hunt began. It was a perfect spring day, bright sunshine and a calm sea as blue as only the Med. can be blue. All the forenoon we held the contact, attacking in turn, and dropping pattern after pattern in thunderous succession. After each one, eyes were trained eagerly aft hoping for wreckage or oil to appear, but none did. By noon, two American destroyers had joined us, and shortly afterwards *Ulster* expended her last depth-charge.

"Proceed to Palermo to replenish," signalled *Laforey*, "then rejoin me at full speed."

We set course for Palermo about 100 miles distant. The last view I had of *Laforey* was of her going in to the attack, with Beaky standing on the bridge bareheaded in the sunshine. I never saw either again. That night in Palermo we intercepted a signal. The U-boat, at long last so damaged by depth-charges that it was obliged to surface, did so at 0110 in the morning. *Laforey's* searchlight was switched on to indicate the surfacing position, and the U-boat actually surfaced in the beam. The ships present opened fire and sank the enemy; but not, unfortunately, before the U-boat skipper had time to fire a torpedo at *Laforey*. He scored a hit, and *Laforey* rolled over and sank almost immediately without a sound.

Unluckily her loss was not at once noticed, owing to the darkness and the rough sea which had just previously got up; in addition, the other destroyers present were for the moment engrossed with the business of picking up the U-boat survivors, of whom twenty-six were saved. When after some appreciable time, it was realised that *Laforey* had sunk also, which was of course completely unexpected, rescue work was much more difficult. Only about sixty or seventy of the destroyer's complement of about two-hundred-and-twenty were picked up, and Beaky was not among them. He was a great loss to the Service.

The U-boat was U 223, and we in *Ulster* were glad to have been the ship to detect it originally and help in its destruction. We were even more thankful when interrogation of survivors revealed that they had been just about to fire a torpedo at us in the first place, when the single depth-charge that we dropped effectively deterred them.

In April, 1944, things were quiet in the Central Mediterranean. In Italy there was a lull in the land fighting, and at sea there was little enemy activity, beyond an occasional U-boat.

For us April included a visit to Sardinia on escort duty, a boiler clean in Naples, and another few days in Capri, by which time the dust had gone; abler pens than mine have described Capri's beauty, and all I can say is that on a spring afternoon in Capri the war seemed a million miles away. But by now our own thoughts were straying constantly away from the Mediterranean to the English Channel. For the talk now was mainly of the forthcoming invasion of Europe. When? Where? And were we going to be "in on it"?

PART FIVE

OPERATION "OVERLORD"

Chapter XIV

STAND BY FOR ACTION

EVEN IN June, 1940, it was obvious that the war would never be won until the British Army marched into Berlin. After Dunkirk, that objective seemed a very long way off: in May 1944, however, the prospects were more encouraging, and preparations to launch the great cross-Channel invasion were now approaching completion. The operation was on an enormous scale, and the problems even more formidable.

The enemy had had nearly four years in which to build up his defences: from Holland to Bay of Biscay, the coast bristled with concrete forts armed with modern guns: the beach-defensive positions were capable of a murderous fire, and mine-fields both on land and in the sea had developed considerably. A long series of Radar stations operated continuously to give warning of impending invasion.

In addition to the above, the enemy knew that the invasion was coming; there could be no concealment of the fact that the whole of the South of England was one enormous armed camp. From the Thames to the Bristol Channel, every port and harbour was crammed with shipping of every sort and size. The major problem—shared by Allies and enemy alike—was WHEN? and WHERE?

The launching of a sea-borne invasion against a heavily-defended coast is such a hazardous affair that the shorter the distance to go by sea the better: the Pas de Calais was the obvious area, and therefore the most heavily defended. In August, 1942, a landing in force, followed by a withdrawal, in the Dieppe area had gained a great deal of experience at heavy cost. The Allies could choose any invasion point from Holland to Brittany: every area had its advantages and disadvantages, and for over two years the problem in all its immensity had been studied.

In May, 1944, everyone knew that the actual area must have been decided upon a long time previously, and that preparations for the assault were working up to a climax. From the experience gained after the landings in North Africa, Sicily, and Italy we all knew that a large naval bombardment force would be required: at Salerno in particular, short range naval gunfire had saved the situation when the issue was largely in doubt. The forthcoming invasion was going to be "the big show" and we all wanted to be there.

One day in Naples, there was a conference of destroyer C.O.'s from the 25th Flotilla in Captain (D)'s cabin on board *Grenville*. The 25th was the "U" Class, and had now built up to its full strength of eight, though the last three to complete building were still in Home waters. They were *Ursa*, *Ulysses* and *Undaunted*.

"Are they going to join us, sir?" I asked. "Or are we going home to join them?"

"Ha, I wonder," replied Captain (D) mysteriously, and said no more on the subject. The discussion continued on a very brand new position-finding apparatus, due to be fitted shortly in our destroyers. I stared rather dumbly at the secret signal.

"But it says this is to be fitted in Lynesse, sir," I said, "surely Lynesse is in Scapa?"

"Exactly," grinned Captain (D), "that is where we are going to find ourselves very shortly."

The next day the four of us—*Grenville*, *Undine*, *Urchin*, and *Ulster*—sailed for Malta. After one night in harbour, in which we said farewell to Malta to no mean tune, we set off at high speed westwards across the Med. in sparkling sunshine, and in an atmosphere of ever-increasing excitement. It was my duty as C.O. to keep our destination to myself: this was rather hard when some boxes of stores prominently labelled "Naval Stores Officer, Scapa" were brought on board shortly before sailing. A brief spell at Algiers to refuel, and then out "through the gate" at Gibraltar into the Atlantic. Four days later, in a horrid cold drizzly dawn, we steamed into Scapa.

We were prepared to find a fair number of ships there, but the total number in harbour was positively staggering. In addition to the Home Fleet, the ships of the D-Day Bombardment Force had started to gather for intensive training. In typical Scapa weather, grey and misty, there were assembled about a dozen heavy ships, a score or more of cruisers and six flotillas of destroyers. That concentration of ships could provide plenty of surprises for the enemy.

There was a pleasant surprise in store for we newcomers from the Mediterranean: after only a couple of days in Scapa, we received orders to sail for Rosyth to give four days' leave to the whole ship's company. It was an extremely well-organised affair. As the four of us secured alongside the pens at daylight, a Care-and-Maintenance party stepped on board each destroyer, all minor problems were brushed aside, and every man Jack of us (nearly 1,000 strong) went ashore over the gangway into a fleet of waiting buses. In no time at all, we were on the train on our way home on leave. It was just like a dream.

It was an odd few days at home. Delight at getting on leave was mingled with the "butterfly-in-the-stomach" feeling of anticipation at the great event so shortly to take place, and for which the whole world was waiting.

"Don't miss the eight o'clock news," I said to my wife, as the evening train steamed northwards out of Carlisle station, "any morning between now and Christmas."

Next morning at eight o'clock, the four destroyers sailed for Scapa: there was a slight hitch when *Grenville* went astern onto a shoal as she slipped from her berth, but she extricated herself, and caught us up as we steamed into the Flow.

During that last week in May the training was intensified to such a pitch that I thought we should all be worn out before the great day even dawned. The main items on the programme were bombardment exercises: these were carried out both by day and night on targets on the islets surrounding Scapa. Army officers were embarked and the firing was conducted in wireless liaison with other Army spotting officers ashore. These exercises were in preparation for the expected occasions after the D-day landing, when naval ships would be called upon to support the troops ashore by gunfire onto enemy targets. "Pin-point accuracy" was the motto, and any other was valueless.

A similar standard was essential for the planned bombardment prior to the actual landing: but in this case, of course, on D-Day itself the spotting would have to be done visually by each ship's individual Gun Control Officer—as the salvos fell: it was not going to be easy by any means. In addition to these firings, we did A.A. practice, night exercises against dummy E-boat attacks (for night patrols off the invasion beaches would be our main duty after D-Day), anti-submarine exercises, and I personally attended umpteen conferences.

At long last came the signal at nine o'clock one morning for "Commanding Officers Only" to open the package containing the details of operation "Overlord". I locked my cabin door, and took the precious envelope gingerly out of my personal safe, where it had simmered for some days. As I spread the chart of the Normandy coast on the table, Georgie leapt up and pawed it, sniffing and purring. After that, I knew all would be well!

If the orders for the Anzio landing had been considerable, those for "Overlord" were ten times as comprehensive. In addition to the main file of overall instructions, there were half a dozen other sealed envelopes with details of all the "sidelines". I put them aside and started wading through the main file: after an hour or so, when I had begun to hoist in some of the salient points, I noticed another envelope labelled "Corrections and Addenda". So I had to get a pen and ink, and start again.

By midday, I was quite exhausted, and also not a little worried. For the orders were all "For Commanding Officer Only", and it did not seem humanly possible for one man to deal with the vast amount of corrections, chart preparation and so on, let alone get a firm grip of the ship's individual duties. Luckily, I was not alone in thinking thus, and within a matter of hours a further signal was received to the effect that "one reliable officer could assist the Commanding Officer". I chose Andrew Gray, and together we battled away sifting the mass of paper, so that those sections affecting *Ulster* could be studied first.

The project was grandiose, to say the least of it. The Normandy beaches had been chosen for the assault: in spite of the long sea passage of nearly a hundred miles, the defences were less strong there, the beaches themselves were sheltered from westerly gales by the Cherbourg peninsula, and it was hoped to capture the port of Cherbourg early on. Moreover, inland

STAND BY FOR ACTION 175

from the beaches, the land was more favourable for the Army breakout.

The size of the initial force to be landed made me gasp. Five divisions of men of a comparative strength of sixty per cent British and Canadian to forty per cent American. There were two Task Forces of ships, the West (American) under Admiral Kirk, U.S.N. and the East (British) under Admiral Vian, R.N. Each Task Force had two sections of the beach labelled from west to east "Utah", "Omaha", "Gold" and "Sword" respectively on a front of about sixty miles from Ouistreham to Carentan and beyond. Each beach had its own special bombardment force, designated by the initial letter of its code word. The total bombardment force was eight heavy ships, twenty-two cruisers, and six flotillas of destroyers, forty-eight ships distributed evenly along the beaches. The 25th Flotilla which included *Ulster* was in Force "G" off "Gold" beach, under Vice-Admiral Dalrymple-Hamilton.

The practical problems facing the actual landing were very worrying. The Channel tides have a large rise-and-fall of nearly twenty feet: thus at low water, an enormous area of beach would be exposed, and to land at that state of tide would be a tremendous ordeal for troops under heavy machine-gun fire. On the other hand, at high tide, the underwater explosive obstacles would be hidden and undoubtedly take a heavy toll of craft and men. H-Hour was finally chosen as three hours before high water: but on such a long stretch of coast, the time of high water varied by more than an hour and a quarter.

To the tidal problem was added that of the moon: D-Day had been chosen during a period of moonlight, since this would greatly help both ships and airborne troops: but only once every month was there a spell of three days when both tides and moon were favourable. The three possible days decided upon for the great assault were June 5th, 6th and 7th: if it did not take place between those dates, a delay of at least two weeks, and possibly a month, was inevitable.

There were to be over 4,000 ships employed in the operation: and the planning required to bring each ship to its own particular destination at its appointed hour necessitated pages of orders. To try and read them all was impossible, nor was it necessary: there was enough to do to try and memorise what was required of *Ulster*.

It was, however, impossible not to be fascinated by such projects as *Mulberry*, the artificial harbours that were to be constructed: *Gooseberries*, the blockships that were to be sunk in line as breakwaters before *Mulberry* was built: *Pluto*, the underwater pipeline which was to be laid to carry petrol from the Isle of Wight to Normandy: the plans to drop three airborne divisions inland behind the German coastal defences at strategic points to prevent reinforcement: the extensive minesweeping operations, involving 350 craft, to sweep and mark ten Channels through the enemy minefields both in mid-Channel and off the beaches: the plans for the colossal bombing assault on the beaches both by R.A.F. and U.S. bombers: and many other stirring sidelines of a smaller, but none the less important nature.

But it was the naval Bombardment which concerned *Ulster*. Every ship had her own target; in brief, the heavy ships and cruisers were entrusted with a coastal battery apiece: these were to be engaged with the help of aerial spotting by observers in Auster aircraft. The destroyers were to take on the coastal defence positions: the whole coast had been photographed from seaward by low-flying aircraft, and every ship was given photos of the particular target she had to engage. The destroyer bombardment would commence with ships at anchor in special positions allotted, about two and a half miles to seaward. Pinpoint accuracy was required here also.

After a certain period of firing, during which time the landing-craft would be manned from the assault ships anchored to seaward, the destroyers were to weigh and close the beach to within a mile range. For this run-in each destroyer was to be preceded by a minesweeper: firing was then to continue at point-blank range and at highest possible rate of fire at the beach defences; all this time the landing craft in their hundreds would be closing in on the beach. The initial bombardment was to continue until the Allied troops were seen to land; then the destroyers were to lie off, and be prepared to repel a heavy air attack: in addition, they were, of course, to continue bombardment at their own discretion, or when ordered by the Senior officers of their Assault Groups.

The operation orders certainly made wonderful reading: I had, naturally, to pass on certain items of information as time went on to the First Lieutenant, the Sub and to Lieutenant Birtwistle, the Gunnery Control officer: but the actual "locale" of invasion I kept dead secret. Local leave was still being granted, and the slightest hint let slip in a moment of careless talk of where or when we might be going could have been disastrous. It amazes me to this day that the overall secrecy was maintained. This was particularly so in the South of England and in the Channel: but here deception was practised on an enormous scale with bogus movements of men ashore, collections of dummy ships in ports along the coast of Kent, aerial reconnaissance in force over the wrong invasion area, and many other ruses. The sum of the whole was that the enemy was convinced that the Allies would land in force in the Pas de Calais.

Meanwhile up in Scapa our training period came to an end, and we lay at our buoys. . . .

> ". . . like greyhounds in the slips,
> Straining upon the start. . . ."

On 29th May, the night before the bombardment forces left Scapa, Admiral Dalrymple-Hamilton invited all the C.O.'s of ships in Force "G" to dinner aboard his flagship the cruiser *Belfast*. It was a very memorable evening. The Admiral had a fine presence, and inspired us all with his cheerful confidence. With a dozen or more of us around his table, we discussed every topic under the sun from China to Peru. But with all his hospitality and the light-hearted badinage that accompanied it, there was a definite pulse-quickening atmosphere of the "eve-of-the-battle".

Next morning the Force was steaming out of harbour and heading south. We were on our way at last.

G

CHAPTER XV

THE DAWN AT LAST

FORCE "G" steamed down the West Coast of Scotland, and up the Firth of Clyde to the Tail o' the Bank. Here we stayed for two days, and it seemed like two weeks to me: the more I studied the orders for the operation the more I wanted to get on with it. Moreover, the strain of keeping secret all that I knew became almost unbearable: I had to be careful every time I spoke, lest I should say even one word which a member of the crew might overhear and pass on to his messmates: not with malice aforethought but through sheer excitement, for on such occasions the habit of "hearing a buzz" dies hard.

The day before sailing, our Gunner, Mr. J. A. Falwell, left the ship to take a special course for promotion to Lieutenant: to our congratulations we added our condolences that he should miss "the big show". Whether he felt the same way about the matter, I do not know.

At last we sailed—officially on exercises—but we all knew pretty well that it was for the real thing: I personally had received a cyphered signal indicating that D-Day would be June 5th. As we steamed down the Firth in a depressing drizzle, I suddenly remembered it was my daughter's sixth birthday. I wondered if I should ever see her again.

The weather continued to be very poor all that day on our way down the Irish Sea. On the morning of the 4th June we found ourselves off the north coast of Somerset, and passing a mixed collection of craft streaming southwards. There was no change in the weather; cold, overcast sky, and what was far worse, a heavy swell coming in from the Atlantic. We were not surprised when orders came that the whole operation had been postponed twenty-four hours, and we reversed course to spend a filthy, boring night tossing about in the Irish Sea. By the next dawn, however, prospects had improved considerably; midday saw us rounding Lands End in bright sunshine and calm sea, and there was no doubt at all then that the show was "on".

As we steamed up Channel that afternoon, from every port and inlet on the South Coast there poured out convoy after convoy of craft of every shape and size, sailing in accordance with the minute to minute programme of the vast operation. There were ships visible in all directions for miles and miles, and it seemed impossible that the enemy could not find out that the invasion forces were on their way at last.

About six p.m. we in *Ulster* were passing close inshore along the Dorset coast. The English countryside was clearly visible in its perfect summer setting; among the checkboard panorama of grassland and crops, the farms and cottages showed up white in the evening sunshine. Little wisps of blue smoke rose vertical from their chimneys in the still, warm air. It was England at her best bidding us all farewell on this great adventure.

And just before dusk there happened something else that was typically English—the Admiral made a signal to his ships in Force "G", the ships who were to do the bombardment next morning. He knew well enough what we were feeling like; he knew if we could batter down the defences before our troops landed, their casualties would be reduced enormously; he knew also that we had no easy task, and that hundreds—if not thousands—of British lives depended on the accuracy of our gunfire. It was a great responsibility for us.

He might have made a long and platitudinous signal, but it so happened that he was a keen cricketer, and his message was short and simple. It read—"*Best of luck to you all. Keep a good length and your eye on the middle stump, and we shall soon have the enemy all out.*"

That was just the sort of signal that was wanted; the sort of signal that made every man say to himself "My God, we will." It made us on board *Ulster* more than ever before determined to put up a good show. Personally I thought it ranked with Nelson's famous signal before Trafalgar.

As darkness fell we were off the Isle of Wight; we turned hard-a-starboard then, and headed for the Normandy beaches ninety miles away. Conditions were perfect; a calm sea and good visibility; moonlight filtered through the clouds sufficiently to give us a clear view under cover of darkness.

"Steady on one eight zero, sir," reported the Coxswain.

Course one eight zero—due south, South for the Coast of France. The die was cast, there was no turning back now.

The excitement on board was intense; men spoke in whispers as though the enemy might hear them ninety miles away; the words of Henry V ran through my mind all night—"Once more unto the breach, dear friends, once more . . ." as the minutes ticked by so appallingly slowly. It seemed an age before we reached the little green flashing dan buoys halfway across, where the swept channels through the minefield started. We glided past the first one, with an M.L. sitting patiently there like a policeman on point duty, and altered course five degrees to starboard.

Apart from the navigational problem, the thought of our task on the morrow weighed heavily on my mind. For the hundredth time I studied the orders under the shaded light of the chart table. We had to anchor literally within yards of our appointed spot, and then knock hell out of those forts: the forts whose photo I had gazed at so often in the last few days. Unless our shells dropped on those two pinpoints on the chart, we would fail in our duty.

If only we weren't mined first! For I remembered some words at the final conference. "The destroyers will lead the way, of course. If the minefield hasn't been properly swept, it will be cheaper to lose a destroyer than a cruiser." *Ulster* was leading one section of Force "G". Slowly the night dragged on. Suddenly the Sub lowered his binoculars and turned to me.

"Land in sight, sir," he said quietly.

My heart gave a great bound as I acknowledged his report. In the first pale light of dawn there before us, a faint low blur on the horizon, lay the coast of France. My mind flashed back to a film called *Came the Dawn*. I had never seen it, but the title fascinated me. For in my own mind I always felt certain that however bad the war news might be, however sick at heart we might get at some awful loss, however long we waited —one day the dawn would come when the Allied Armies set foot in France. For four years the enemy had held the whole

Atlantic seaboard from Norway to Spain; for four years, aided by his U-boats, this awful menace had hung over us like a permanent black cloud; for four years, also, millions had waited, desperate for this dawn, the dawn that would lead to their liberation.

WELL, HERE IT WAS AT LAST!

The tension on board was terrific, and as if to encourage us even more, a continual roar of aircraft passed overhead southwards—our own bombers going to play their part. The daylight seemed to come up much quicker now; on either side of us, the faint outlines of hundreds of ships could be made out, steaming placidly along in an orderly array according to plan. It was a magnificent sight, almost unbelievable in its imperturbability; it was Sea Power personified.

As we approached the coast we overtook several convoys of smaller craft, and had a hectic few minutes weaving our way through them; we could not stop as the other ships were close astern of us. Some of these tiny craft were all over the shop, and we whizzed past with only a few yards to spare. I saw a brass-hatted officer stand up and shake his fist at me!

And then quite suddenly it was broad daylight; houses and forts on the coast ahead of us were plainly visible. A lighthouse, yellow in the light of dawn, stood there like a friendly finger to beckon us in. It was a perfect June morning quiet and still. On either beam the other destroyers were forming up in a long line, and astern of us the cruisers were easing down preparatory to dropping anchor; they were going to fire over our heads. My watch showed five past five; not long to go now. The immediate problem was to get plumb into the right spot before anchoring.

"Nearly there, sir. Steer two degrees to starboard for three minutes."

From the chart table the Sub's voice was muffled, but he could not conceal his excitement. Other reports followed in quick succession.

"Main armament ready, sir!"

"Starboard anchor ready, sir!"

Once again I gazed at the typed orders beside me. The whole thing was working out fine to date.

"Turn to anchor now, sir!"

I gazed at the other destroyers. Yes, they were turning also, we were hunky-dory. I turned the *Ulster* beam on to the beach, now less than three miles away, and we let go the anchor underfoot. It was to help keep the ship steady during the bombardment.

"Well, boys," I said, "we've arrived."

The director and the guns trained round. Ten past five, only a few minutes now. The silence was uncanny, almost disappointing. We had expected to be met with a hail of gunfire, and a rain of bombs, but nothing had happened. It was like a peacetime exercise, but all the same, I found myself shivering violently. It seemed very cold at anchor.

Half a minute to go. My heart was thumping like the proverbial sledge-hammer.

"STAND BY!"

As I gave the order with my eyes glued to my stopwatch, my thoughts flashed for just that brief interval to my little country home, four hundred miles away. Five fifteen; all would be quiet there, too. My wife and little girl still fast asleep upstairs in their bedroom, and David the Sealyham downstairs curled up in the kitchen chair. Outside in the garden with the Lake District Hills all round, it would be fresh and cool, the birds cheeping in the appletrees, and the old tabby puss (Georgie's mum) gazing at them enviously as she picked her way daintily across the dewy lawn—the same perfect June morning, I could see it all.

"OPEN FIRE!"

For one hour and ten minutes we fired without ceasing, in one long, magnificent and exhilarating roar. At intervals throughout, the signalman touched my sleeve and held up a signal for me to read. Halfway through, he showed me one that has been made many times in British Naval history. . . .

"Engage The Enemy More Closely."

At that signal all the destroyers weighed anchor, and moved closer inshore, each one led by their own individual minesweeper in a single combined line. We were firing as fast as we could now, almost point blank at the shore defences. The assault craft, full of soldiers, were passing us on their way into the assault; we could see the men in them, crouched down

ready to spring ashore. In one boat a man was standing up
playing the bagpipes.

For five minutes, just ahead of them and just before they
landed, there was a trememdous shower of rockets onto the
nearby beach defences from craft specially designed to fire
them, and then on "Gold" beach, at half past six on that
June morning, in the centre sectors of that great assault, the
British armies returned to France. One of the greatest moments
in history—one the whole free world was waiting for—had
arrived at last.

From the bridge of the *Ulster*, we had a grandstand view
of the whole proceeding, and it was a magnificent and im-
pressive sight. We ceased firing just then, and moved out to
seaward to wait the air attack that never came. We anchored,
and a small craft came back alongside with some men that
had been picked up from the sea. Doc Johnston dealt with them
quietly and quickly.

Up on the bridge we looked at each other, not knowing
what to say. The bombardment was over, we had done our
best. I picked up the telephone to the director tower.

"Bertie?"

"Yes, sir."

"Pass to all positions from the Captain—Well done, everybody."

"Aye, aye, sir. Thank you, sir."

I could hear the message being relayed to all the guns, and
a muffled cheer came up from "B" gun's crew. I crawled
stiffly to the engine-room phone.

"Chief?"

"Yes, sir."

"Pass to all positions—The bombardment seems to have
gone off well, the troops are going ashore in thousands: and
tell your chaps from me they've done damn well."

"Aye, aye, sir. Thank you, sir."

After a short interval we relaxed somewhat, and some of
the crew went to have breakfast. Up on the bridge there
was a great silence among us still up there. It was only then
that the strain and excitement of the last twelve hours began to
tell. The Sub crouched over the chart, grey with fatigue, and
the signalman leant against the side of the bridge, struggling

to keep his eyes open. Perched on a couple of chairs beside the compass, and blinking stupidly like owls disturbed in daylight, the Officer of the Watch and I listened as best we could to the progress of the battle ashore; the crackling messages in the R/T set were like a running commentary of some great event. I was so utterly weary that I just could not think about anything.

It was five past eight when Number One came up to take over the forenoon watch.

"Well, it's on the news, sir—the folks at home will have got their thrill all right this morning."

The folks at home! I could see them in my home, I could see them in a million homes, I could picture the excitement and the jubilation everywhere, the calling out of windows to friends passing, the chatter between complete strangers in trains and buses. . . .

"We've landed!"

Even more vividly could I picture the receipt of the news on secret sets in a million homes and places still under the heel of the hated Nazi. . . . Then Number One's voice broke in on my thoughts once more.

"It looks as though we've managed it all right, sir," he added quietly.

Even then it took a few minutes for the meaning of his words to sink in properly. After four years, the dawn had come at last, and victory was ours; the day was won, the Army had landed on the shores of France. For whatever the future held in store, whatever setbacks there were to come, however hard the fighting might be, the first and hardest hurdle had been jumped that morning—D-Day, the sixth of June, 1944.

I will never forget the intensity of that moment on the bridge of the *Ulster* just then. I was overwhelmed by a surge of emotion that swept into oblivion any trace of weariness. It was a moment when the memories of every past triumph, every thrill of accomplishment, and every glow of happiness combined in one great brilliant flash. It was the most wonderful moment of my whole life. But outstanding in that surge of emotion was heartfelt thankfulness and pride. Thankfulness to the Almighty for granting us the victory, and pride in our Service and our native land.

In due course, however, mental exhilaration was inevitably followed by physical exhaustion. Fifteen hours of non-stop concentrated excitement produced a state of complete and utter weariness.

"Take the weight, will you?" I said to Number One, "I simply must have a few minutes shut-eye."

I staggered off the bridge and had only just slumped down on my sea cabin bunk, with a nervous but purring Georgie beside me, when the bell went again.

"Signal to proceed on patrol as previously ordered, sir."

I swore heartily.

"O.K.—start weighing. I'll be up when I can."

Although the initial landing had obviously gone more or less according to plan, there was no time to sit back and congratulate ourselves. The "build up" ships were streaming in, and they had to be protected both by sea and from the air; the enemy soon started to hit back hard.

Ulster was one of the many destroyers that endeavoured to form a steel ring to seaward of the beaches to protect the ships from E-boat and U-boat attacks. These patrols, particularly at night, were no picnic as they were on a line parallel to the beach, and hence at right angles to the stream of incoming and outgoing traffic. By day we moved up and down, awaiting calls for bombardment of targets ashore through the co-operation of Army spotting officers. This was another typical instance of the value of sea power; for while the German positions were still within our range, bombardments from seaward were carried out continuously. For several days after D-Day, the cruisers and battleships were able to send salvos of heavy shells far inland onto such targets as concentrations of enemy troops or tanks.

The few days immediately following the landing were very strenuous, and after we had moved about all along the beaches without coming to any harm it is possible that I may have got a bit careless, or tired, or both. Anyhow, what happened on the morning of June 9th was entirely my fault, and I have never tried to disguise the fact.

It was a dull and wet morning; we had been on the "qui vive" all night due to various alarms and excursions, and about seven o'clock we were ordered to the eastern edge of "Gold" beach to carry out a bombardment. We set off, and got all ready to open fire. A tremendous number of small craft were milling about in the anchorage, and I was more engrossed in avoiding them than in paying attention to our actual position.

Before we pinpointed ourselves on the chart, I steered an approximate course to the Eastward; as we steamed along, a destroyer to seaward called us by lamp, but just as the duty signalman started to answer her, the *Rodney* from a position inshore called us also.

"Answer *Rodney*," I snapped to the signalman, "tell the destroyer to wait."

"Close me," sang out the signalman, reading *Rodney's* message. I altered course slightly to starboard to do so, and the man turned his attention to the destroyer, still flashing angrily . . .

"*Ulster* from C.-in-C.—" he started chanting in the usual sing-song employed by his branch, but he got no further, for just then the *Rodney* called us again.

"Take *Rodney* now," I ordered.

He did so, and reported her message—"Despatch is necessary."

I nodded acknowledgement, for my attention was rivetted on a line of minesweepers approaching dangerously close to port. As I watched them, I sang out down the voicepipe to the wheelhouse.

"One eight zero revolutions!"

Ulster leapt forward through the water like a dog when its collar is released; I was just noting with satisfaction that we would draw clear of the minesweepers, when there was a most terrible crash, and the whole ship shuddered in an appalling manner.

"STOP BOTH ENGINES!"

My first impression was that we had been mined, as the bump was reminiscent of the *Black Swan* affair. I ran to the side of the bridge and looked over. Mud and sand were boiling up to the surface of the water, and then I realised with horror the terrible truth.

"We're aground!"

I felt absolutely sick with shame and anger.

"Where the hell are we, Sub?" I shouted down to the charthouse, where he had taken the chart to keep it dry.

"Just fixing us now, sir."

The irony of his remark failed to register. We were fixed all right. His bearings of two churches put us dangerously close to the end of a reef called the Point d'Essein, jutting out from the mouth of a little river. It was patently obvious that, judging for a certain amount of error in his bearings, that was where we were all right—on the tip of the reef. A glance at the tide tables showed us that it was dead low water.

"Oh hell!"

I knew at once that the ship must have been damaged underwater; we had been brought up more or less all standing from nearly twenty knots. I gave orders for the engines not to be moved on any account, and went down below to inspect the damage. To my amazement no flooding was reported, and returning on deck I found a small tug had materialised from nowhere, and was getting a wire onto our stern to pull us off. In about half an hour we floated clear, and everyone breathed again. Then the engines were tried very slowly, the starboard one first; the shaft revolved normally until 140 revs were reached, then an unusual vibration crept in; still, that was not too bad. The port shaft made the most horrible noises as soon as we started up, so we did not try it again. As it subsequently turned out that the propellor was completely wiped off, the fact was not surprising!

Meanwhile, the signalman had taken in the message that the destroyer to seaward was trying to pass to us before. It was an immediate signal ordering us to return to Portsmouth to refuel and reammunition. If only we had received it a few minutes earlier, we would have been steaming joyfully northwards across the Channel to England, Home and Beauty instead of aground off the French coast in disgrace. IF ONLY . . . The two saddest words in any language in the world.

We went astern into deep water, and reported the situation to one and all. The news was not exactly received with enthusiasm, and after hanging about for a few hours like a schoolboy waiting to be caned by the headmaster, we were ordered to join up with a small convoy returning to the Portsmouth area. We crept into Spithead after dark in hangdog fashion, and anchored near the depot-ship *Tyne*. Next day divers reported that the starboard propellor was badly chipped, and that the port one was conspicuous by its absence.

After a good deal of discussion, it was decided to repair the ship at Cardiff; we were towed round there by a minute tug. The ignominy of this proceedings was only exceeded by the qualms felt at being towed at slow speed on a steady course through the English Channel, a sitting shot for any U-boats or E-boats. Luckily their attention must have been concentrated on the French coast, for we arrived safely on June 22nd.

A Court of Inquiry was held over the circumstances of our grounding. I subsequently received from the Admiralty a somewhat frosty letter to the effect that I was to blame (an opinion with which I entirely agreed) and that I was to be more careful in future.

"Cheer up," said an Admiral I met later, "no man's a real sailor till he's run a ship ashore. We all make mistakes now and then; I can tell you that before the war I ran a damn cruiser on the rocks in the West Indies. She's still there!"

My friend and fellow C.O., Leonard was even more encouraging.

"Run aground?" he said, "lucky chap. You'll now get six month's cushyarse job ashore, and a brass hat at the end of it!"

Repairs to the *Ulster* took longer than was anticipated, and three months later she was still sitting in Cardiff. She was destined for the Far East when ready for sea again, but as this time approached I knew in my own mind I was not really confident enough to take her out there. Continuous seagoing command for over three-and-a-half years under wartime conditions, plus the additional experience of having run aground, had had their effect on me. I had spells of sleep walking (twice in harbour I found myself on the bridge in the middle of the night in my pyjamas, under the impression that we were at sea!) and I began to worry unduly about the prospects of handling the ship.

It was clearly my duty to ask to be relieved of my command, much as it went against the grain to do so, and in due course I wrote officially to Captain (D). He expressed his regret,

but agreed entirely with me. So one day Lieutenant Commander R. J. Hanson, D.S.O., D.S.C. turned up in Cardiff to
take over the ship; he had had *Ulysses* for some time, but she
had been damaged by a fire in dock.

"I hope you like cats," I said, "because Georgie goes where
Ulster goes."

I was very sorry to leave *Ulster* and her officers and men;
and if my wife smokes too much today, it is because she has
a very smart silver cigarette-case with the ship's crest, the
"Red Hand of Ulster" engraved on it, which was a present
to her from the wardroom, greatly appreciated by us both;
and I have a little tray with the signatures of the officers and
Chiefs and P.O.'s thereon and Georgie's paw mark which I
value just as much.

It had been a great year in *Ulster*, a very eventful one, despite
the fact that the ship had been rather badly knocked about three
times—once honourably, once accidentally, and once due
to my carelessness. But *Humanum est Errare*, and the compensation was the fact that "we were there" for D-Day. For I
personally shall always consider that the 6th June, 1944, was one
of the greatest days in the history of the Navy, the British
nation, and even of the whole free world.

Be that as it may, I shall always remember with a glow
of humble pride one paragraph in the orders for Operation
"Overlord". It read as follows:

"It is the primary duty of the Navy to ensure that the
Army is landed safely on the shores of France. Regardless
of any difficulties encountered, or losses sustained, this will
be done".

It was.

WAR TO PEACE

CHAPTER XVI

EASTWARD HO!

M Y FRIEND Leonard was not far wrong in his forecast: after a pleasant six months ashore on the Staff of C.-in-C., Rosyth, I was appointed Commander of H.M.S. *Glengyle*: the job carried an acting "brass hat", but I viewed the prospect with little enthusiasm. I joined the ship at the Tail o' the Bank on the Clyde in June, 1945, when the rejoicings after "VE Day" had been replaced by the realisation that the battle against the Japanese still had to be won. It was a sombre thought.

Glengyle was a 10,000-ton merchant ship, converted to accommodate about 1,000 soldiers, and to carry twenty-four landing craft to put them ashore for an assault. Her initial conversion had cost an immense amount of money—the forward holds had been turned into messdecks for the ship's company, and her after ones into the same to take the military personnel. They were pretty uncomfortable as all of them, except one right aft, had no portholes. Extra cabins had been built for the ship's officers, and three large "dormitories" for the Army officers. *Glengyle* had had a very distinguished career throughout the earlier years of the war, all round the Mediterranean—including the Greece and Crete campaigns— and at Dieppe.

Some of her officers had served in her the whole war. Among them was the Engineer Officer, Lieutenant Commander William Topley, R.N.R., a very fine officer and most likeable shipmate; the wartime steaming record of the ship—125,000 miles under all sorts of conditions of weather and operational requirements—bore eloquent testimony to his efficiency. The Paymaster, Lieutenant Commander Wood, R.N.R., was an enormous help to me in the complex problems of victualling and supply that arose every day. The Electrical Officer, an ex-P. and O. officer serving as a Lieutenant R.N.R. under the T. 124X agreement, was "Sandy" Sanderson—a "live wire" in every direction.

The rest of the wardroom consisted of every possible sort and size of officer—R.N., R.N.R., R.N.V.R., R.N.R. (T124X), Royal Marines—but despite many problems, we seemed to pull along together fairly well. *Glengyle* had had several Commanding Officers: the one who took over the ship just after I joined was Captain B. B. Grant, R.D., R.N.R., a man whom we all liked and respected greatly.

In June, 1945, even more extensive alterations had just been carried out in *Glengyle*. She had been prepared as a Headquarters Ship for further landings in the Far East; many more cabins had been built in, plus extensive wireless offices and gunnery equipment.

Those of us in the know realised that our first job was going to be operation "Zipper", the landing in Malaya planned for that autumn. As a Headquarters Ship designate, we carried in addition a number of additional officers, including Captain J. P. de W. Kitcat, D.S.O., R.N. who was Senior Officer of an Assault Group.

The preparation and orders for "Zipper" were no less comprehensive than those for "Overlord", which exactly a year previously, in this very same spot, had produced such an atmosphere of tense anticipation for all of us on board *Ulster*. 1944 —France: 1945—Malaya: 1946—Japan? (When, I thought to myself, will all this ever end?). Moreover, in addition, I had to deal with the thousand-and-one problems of a large ship newly commissioned, and to make arrangements for the 600 parachutists whom we were taking on passage to Bombay.

During our last fortnight in the Clyde I only managed to get ashore twice; the fact that the weather was perfect made staying on board even more annoying. About two days before sailing, I took a boat over to Helensburgh, got on my bike and rode over the hill to the Fruin valley and down to Loch Lomond. For an hour or so I sat by the shores of the loch, completely happy in the beauty of the scene, and wondering if I should ever see it again.

We sailed at dawn on 27th July, and I do not think I have ever felt so depressed in all my life. The natural heartache of leaving home and family, and the thought of sailing ten thousand miles to grapple with an enemy even more bestial than the one we had fought for nearly six years in Europe, combined to fill me with utter gloom. I have no doubt that everyone on board felt much the same way that morning.

It was not a happy trip out: with an overcrowded ship many problems arose, not the least of which was the question of fresh water. With an overall complement of 1,000 on board the fresh water consumption rose to staggering heights: when we reached the Red Sea, neither the distilling machinery nor the men manning it could stand the pace, and we had to ration fresh water, with resultant moans and groans from everyone. However, on the night of 6th August I was on the bridge when an excited signalman came up.

"Wunnerful noos on the wireless, sir," he gabbled, "one of them noo attyomic bombs dropped in Japan—wiped out the 'ole city—'Iroshima, they called it."

I accepted the story with reserve; little did I think that within six months I would be standing in a plain of flat rubble that had once been that same city. But three days later, there was similar news of the next bomb at Nagasaki, and when in due course we arrived in Bombay one steaming, muggy dawn, the place was full of rumours. The very next morning, as we lay at anchor in sheets of torrential rain, the "victory signal" arrived.

I happened to be in my cabin when a copy was brought to me. I just could not believe it; for a long time I sat staring out of the porthole, and muttering "Thank God for that!" Then from the nearest ship, only just visible through the downpour, I saw little wisps of steam dribbling out of her siren: soundless to start with, then growing in volume. Puff— puff—puff—BOOM. . . ."

The letter "V". "V" for Victory at last!

Soon every ship in the anchorage joined in: it was like the zoo at feeding time. Then came the anti-climax—another signal to *Glengyle*.

"Stand by (it read) to embark 1,000 commando troops for passage to Trincomalee. Ship is to sail immediately they are embarked".

Operation "Zipper" it appeared was still on. At Trincomalee we found assembled a huge force of ships, loaded and ready: but in due course, "Zipper" in its original form was cancelled, and *Glengyle* was ordered to Hong Kong. We arrived there on September 8th, and the Commandos went ashore as the first garrison. Hong Kong was like a city of the dead: dirt and drabness was the overall impression after nearly four years of Japanese occupation. A big squadron of British ships lay at anchor in the harbour, and Admiral Sir Cecil Harcourt was Acting Governor.

On 16th September the Japanese formally surrendered in Hong Kong. Commanding Officers of H.M. Ships in harbour and many other senior officers were invited to be present. It was a terribly hot day, very unsuitable for wearing tunics and long trousers.

The surrender took place in Government House in the large circular white-walled main hall; on the parquet flooring a dark carpet had been spread with a table in the centre, and at intervals around the hall were Royal Marine sentries with pistols. The more senior officers were formed up in an orderly array at one end of the hall, while the main body of spectators were up on the gallery above. When all was set, Admiral Harcourt entered from a door on the far side, and in a moment or two, the Japanese leaders came in from another entrance, escorted by an officer. For a little while there was dead silence. It was a dramatic moment.

Then the terms of the surrender were read out and translated by an interpreter. The Japanese nodded in agreement, took off their swords and placed them on the table; that gesture must have hurt them more than anything else, and doubtless everyone present secretly hoped it did. Then the Japanese signed the agreement in turn; this was a longish process, as they did so with the usual little brush, and then each man added his own personal "chop" with a die produced from his pocket, and using some wax that was on the table.

Admiral Harcourt then signed, and stood up as if to signify that that was all. The Japanese bowed, still with impassive faces, and were marched out again. There was a pause, and then the Admiral made for the other door; as he did so, every-one present came to the salute. At the door he turned round, returned the salute with a grave smile, and then went out. The war was over.

But there was still plenty to be done. The same evening on board *Glengyle* we received a signal, asking how many civilian internees we could embark for passage to England. We replied that we could manage fifty men and seventy-five women and children. Then we sat back and awaited events.

"We're going to have some fun", I said to Flags.

"Fun, sir?" he replied, "This isn't my idea of fun."

He showed me another signal.

Glengyle from C.-in-C. (I read) Stand by to embark 980 Indian troops for passage to Bombay.

I nearly threw a fit: luckily the second signal was cancelled, and a nominal list of internees for passage was soon forthcoming. Many of them I had known in pre-war days. The next day a minesweeper went round to Stanley Bay and embarked these folk from their wartime jail, starting about 9 a.m. By noon, the ship had steamed back into Hong Kong, and was alongside the jetty where *Glengyle* was berthed; an hour later they were all safely aboard our ship, and we were heading out to sea with the knowledge that our guests, and possibly ourselves, were homeward bound. It was a memorable experience.

As we were steaming out of harbour, I chanced to go right aft. An elderly man was standing alone by the ensign staff gazing at the British Fleet anchored in the brilliant sunshine. The tears were streaming down his cheeks.

"The White Ensign's back at last," he said, "how we've all waited for this day."

I thought of his remark eighteen months later when I took the brand new destroyer *Concord* into Hong Kong harbour; the scene was much the same.

But there was no time for tears on board *Glengyle* just then: the trip was labelled (by me) operation "Joyride" and we did our best to make it so. It was a truly remarkable situation for all concerned: those who had endured three-and-a-half years of hell in Stanley Jail under the Japanese now found themselves in the twinkling of an eye on board one of H.M. Ships: we, who had battled away through five-and-a-half years of war, were suddenly confronted with a peacetime passenger ship routine. For the next ten days all thoughts of work went overboard.

The children came off best of all. Swings, rocking-horses and a canvas bath on the upper deck appeared in no time. One of the messdecks was turned into a cinema, and some of the young children were introduced for the first time to Donald Duck and his gang. The grown-ups did not fare so badly either. The first night at sea I sent for our wine steward.

"Peace time now. Open the bar tonight from six till eight."

"Very good, sir."

The next morning someone said to me—"Look, sir, must we shut the bar at eight? These folk haven't had a party for three-and-a-half years."

The night after that, or, to be more accurate, the morning after the night after, the bar shut at 2 a.m.

I had secretly worried slightly about the food question; would we have enought meat and enough variety from the usual war-time "scrag end"? I need not have worried at all; most of our guests were quite content with the simplest fare.

"Bread and butter," said one lady, "do you know, I have seen nothing so marvellous for years as those plates of white bread and dishes of butter on the table."

Most of our guests put on a pound in weight for every day aboard; the combination of a normal diet and sea air brought about almost miraculous results; maybe the general air of happiness had something to do with it as well, for the trip was in Naval parlance just one long party. And so it went on. We had hoped that we were to take our guests all the way to England, but the Powers-that-Be said not, and we received orders to transfer them to the P. and O. *Maloja* at Colombo. On 26th September we arrived at Colombo at daybreak, the best time to arrive at that wonderful harbour, one of the most fascinating in the world. There were large numbers of ships lying at the buoys, and a glance through binoculars told me there was unusual activity for that early hour.

"They've got the Guard and Band out for us, anyhow," remarked somebody as we passed in through the entrance.

So they had. On the centre breakwater, only a few yards from the ship's side as we glided past, was a Royal Marine Band playing "John Peel". From that moment we never

looked back that day. For as *Glengyle's* stem passed the breakwater, there broke out in the harbour a schemozzle that was
"V-J Day" all over again. "V's" were sounded on sirens,
the signal "Welcome" was hoisted in flags at all yardarms,
and on many an upperdeck there were crowds of men waving
and cheering.

One of the older lady passengers touched my arm.

"What's all this for?" she asked.

It was some time before I could answer. Then——

"It's for you," I said.

We had a very hectic forenoon transferring our guests to
the *Maloja*, and later in the evening a dozen of us from the
wardroom went over in a couple of landing craft, to bid them
a final farewell just before sailing. There were a good many
kisses and a few suspiciously bright eyes about.

As the *Maloja* slipped from her buoys, and glided slowly
towards the breakwater we escorted her out in the landing
craft; a final wave and a cheer then we returned to the *Glengyle*.
Operation "Joyride" was over.

It was remarkably flat and quiet when we got back inboard; the wardroom was deserted, and we dispersed dejectedly
to our respective cabins. I knew that in mine a great stack
of paper work, long neglected, required immediate attention.

But oddly enough, I never got down to it just then. For
there were some other letters on my desk that were far more
interesting.

". . . on behalf of all the men passengers . . . our sincere
thanks to you all aboard *Glengyle* . . . for making this last week
so memorable . . . Signed Cyril Brown, Lionel MacRae."

". . . on behalf of all the women ex-internees . . . our most
grateful thanks to all of you for all your kindness . . . Signed
Joan Smalley, Margaret Hearson."

". . . you and your shipmates have made these last few
days some of the happiest and most unforgettable . . . Signed
Freddie."

There were several others. I sat there for quite a time reading
them through. The atmosphere did not seem quite so flat
after all.

As the first notes of the "Sunset" call floated in through my
port, I picked my cap up and went out on deck; far out to the

westward, the sun gave a final goodnight wink as it dived into the sea, and for a moment the ships and the whole harbour were bathed in a brilliant golden glow.

As I stood there at the salute, while the music of the bugle and the shrill notes of the boatswains' pipes echoed across the harbour, I too experienced a glow of supreme happiness. For while operation "Joyride" might never be recorded in the annals of Naval History, it would be recorded as a proud and happy memory in the minds of all those who took part in it.

"CARRY ON!"

The two notes of the bugle and the saucy chirrup of the pipes rang out on all sides; then, as if worked by a giant master switch, the lights went on in every ship in harbour. The soft, warm darkness soon disguised the grey paint and the warlike silhouettes; I saw once again the Colombo that I had so often gazed upon as a midshipman, fifteen years before, from the deck of the *Emerald* lying at these same buoys: a harbour once more full of ships "passing upon the seas upon their lawful occasions".

Moreover, not only in Colombo but all over the world in countless hearts and homes and harbours, after six years of darkness, the light of hope had been switched on once again.

I stood there for quite some time with my thoughts—thankful and happy, humble and yet not a little proud.